Imperishable Beauty

Imperishable Beauty
Art Nouveau Jewelry

Yvonne J. Markowitz and Elyse Zorn Karlin

with contributions by Susan Ward

LH

Lund Humphries

CONTENTS

Fig. 1
Dante Gabriel Rossetti
Bocca Baciata, 1859
oil on panel

DIRECTOR'S FOREWORD

Art Nouveau jewelry is often described as the most tantalizing, exotic, and technically sophisticated adornment ever created. It is characterized by whiplash curves, asymmetrical design, a pastel palette, and vivid imagery. The ingenious artists who designed and fabricated these extraordinary works often experimented with exciting new materials, magically transforming mundane substances into bold, sensuous forms and phantasmagorical scenes. Creatures of the night, human hybrids, and meandering vines impart an edgy sensibility, while luminous dragonflies and shimmering lily pads evoke the vitality of the untamed pond.

Art Nouveau was primarily a European movement, with France and Belgium leading the way in this bold new aesthetic. Across the Atlantic, in the Americas, the exaggerated forms were more modest and attenuated. However, with its emphasis on traditional materials and handwork, the style would influence several generations of jewelers in the studio jewelry movement.

The adornments in *Imperishable Beauty: Art Nouveau Jewelry* come from one private American collection. Assembled over the course of nearly five decades, it ranks foremost in its depth and breadth and testifies to the collectors' passion and their discriminating taste.

MALCOLM ROGERS
Ann and Graham Gund Director
Museum of Fine Arts, Boston

ACKNOWLEDGMENTS

The authors are indebted to many individuals whose efforts made this publication and the accompanying exhibition possible. At the Museum of Fine Arts, Boston, we wish to thank Malcolm Rogers, Katherine Getchell, and Pamela Parmal for their enthusiasm and support. We are grateful for Mark Polizzotti's expert guidance in shaping the book and for Sarah McGaughey Tremblay's sensitive and thoughtful editing. The photographic skills of Greg Heins and the design talent of Cynthia Randall greatly enhanced the publication, while the production work of Terry McAweeney and Jodi Simpson assisted in bringing the book to press. Our colleagues in various departments graciously offered us their advice and expertise. They include George Shackelford, Tracey Albainy, Marietta Cambareri, and Meghan Melvin in Art of Europe; Clifford Ackley, Stephanie Stepanek, and Patrick Murphy in Prints, Drawings, and Photographs; Gerry W. R. Ward and Kelly L'Ecuyer in Art of the Americas; Anne Morse, Sarah Thompson, and Abraham Schroeder in Art of Asia, Oceania, and Africa; Rita Freed, Lawrence Berman, and Joyce Haynes in Art of the Ancient World; Lauren Whitley, Alex Huff, and Hillary Kidd in Textile and Fashion Arts; Joan Wright, Annette Manick, Richard Newman, Susanne Gansicke, and Martha Shaw in Conservation and Collections Management; and Patrick McMahon, Danielle Berger, and Jaime Roark in Exhibitions and Design. As in many Museum projects, the behind-the-scenes efforts of volunteers also proved invaluable. Jeweler Toni Strassler offered countless hours and technical insights, while Sheila Shear lent her organizational skills and Steve Schirra assisted in the book's production process.

We also extend our gratitude to many outside the Museum who generously provided information and advice. They include the decorative arts scholars Janet Zapata; Diana Scarisbrick; Ulysses Dietz, of the Newark Museum of Art; and Katherine Purcell, of Wartski, London. Sonya and David Newell-Smith, of the Tadema Gallery, London, generously offered us images for reproduction. Very special thanks go to Gloria Lieberman, head of the jewelry department at Skinner Auctioneers, Boston, for providing partial funding of the publication. We are also grateful to Susan B. Kaplan for her generous support and encouragement. And finally, we thank Joseph and Ruth Sataloff, collectors extraordinaire and tireless educators, who willingly share their expertise with all those who love the jeweled arts. We are among the many who have benefited from their lifelong commitment to jewelry scholarship.

YVONNE J. MARKOWITZ
ELYSE ZORN KARLIN

ART NOUVEAU JEWELRY: AN OVERVIEW

Yvonne J. Markowitz

The jewelry created in Europe at the turn of the twentieth century represented an exciting new aesthetic. Flamboyant and fantastical, it was characterized by sensuous forms, dramatic imagery, and a vivid, poetic symbolism. It was, in large measure, a reaction against mainstream historicism, growing industrialization, and the "tyranny of the diamond."[1]

The designers and jewelers who produced these ornaments were part of an international movement known as Art Nouveau, which originated in France and Belgium and spread as far as the Americas and Russia. This decorative new style, with its sinuous, asymmetrical lines and organic forms, was adopted by artists in many media but found its fullest expression in the decorative arts, poster art, and, to a lesser extent, architecture. Although the style varied in its different manifestations, the artists involved were united in their quest to break with the past and reinvigorate what they viewed as stagnant design.

Many of the jewelry makers who adopted the new style acquired their skills in traditional, high-style jewelry houses but looked elsewhere for inspiration. Like other Art Nouveau artists, they found it in the work of the Pre-Raphaelites, the philosophies of John Ruskin and William Morris, the paintings and poems of the Symbolists, and the arts of Japan. And although they had a keen interest in the natural world, they rejected the rigid, unimaginative naturalism typical of nineteenth-century European decorative arts, choosing to interpret nature rather than imitate it.

Sources of Inspiration

During the mid-nineteenth century, a group of English poets, painters, and critics had resolved to redefine and revitalize the arts. Known as the Pre-Raphaelite Brotherhood, they rejected the mechanistic realism of the Royal Academy and looked toward medieval culture and the art of the Italian quattrocento for inspiration. For them, art was a spiritual and moral endeavor that had profound social, aesthetic, and cultural ramifications. They believed strongly in the unity of the arts and felt that a holistic approach was compromised by the increased compartmentalization of everyday life, as society became more and more industrialized. In an effort to restore truth to art, Dante Gabriel Rossetti, Edward Burne-Jones, and other painters embraced a heightened awareness of nature and an almost obsessive attention to detail, abandoning conventional methods of representation and adopting flatter planes with greater surface decoration. They experimented with pigments and glazes that made many of their paintings appear jewel-like (fig. 1, p. 4).[2] The female figure, romanticized and eroticized, was a popular Pre-Raphaelite subject, made even more provocative through the artists' liberal use of symbolism. Burne-Jones, in particular, imbued his women with a sensual, dreamy languor (fig. 2). This fascination with nature and the feminine would later resonate with Art Nouveau artists.

When the work of the Pre-Raphaelites was criticized as being primitive, emotionally charged, and

1. Notes begin on page 163.

Fig. 2
Sir Edward Coley Burne-
Jones (English, 1833–1898),
Hope, 1896, oil on canvas

Fig. 3 (opposite, detail)
William Morris (English,
1834–1896), *Length of furnishing fabric: "Cray,"* about 1884,
block-printed cotton plain
weave

excessively morbid, the influential British critic John Ruskin came to its defense. A personal
friend of Rossetti, Ruskin was an artist-poet
who wrote extensively on the nature of art and
society. He was keenly aware of the sociopoliti-
cal ramifications of industrialization, attribut-
ing "the decay of art to the fact that the modern
factory, with its mechanical mode of production and division of labour, prevents a genuine
relationship between the worker and his work;
that is to say, it crushes out the spiritual element and estranges the producer from the
product of his hands."[3] He applauded the Pre-
Raphaelites for their desire to unite the arts
and for their rejection of the artificial distinc-
tion between fine and applied art.

Like the Pre-Raphaelites, Ruskin was an
admirer of medieval art, and he encouraged the
revival of the Gothic style. Originally confined
to religious sculpture and architecture, the
Gothic style had spread quickly in Europe during the twelfth to fifteenth centuries with the
rise of cities, universities, and bourgeois
patrons. For Ruskin, the pointed arches, ribbed
vaults, and emotionally charged spaces of the
architecture represented solidarity, aspiration,
and honesty of construction. He also held
medieval guilds in high regard, as these asso-
ciations of skilled craftsmen promoted and
celebrated time-honored crafts. By the 1880s,
artists in England began experimenting with
a modified form of the guild system. These
groups were intent on creating humanistic
environments for artists and stressed individuality rather than standardization in the production of everyday objects.

Ruskin's ideas greatly influenced William
Morris, a socially conscious artist and friend of

Fig. 4
Utagawa Hiroshige I
(Japanese, 1797–1858),
The Iris Garden at Horikiri,
1857, woodblock print

Rossetti and Burne-Jones. Morris advanced Ruskin's principles in the decorative arts as a leader in the emerging Arts and Crafts movement in Great Britain. Proponents of this movement championed design reform and the elevation of handicraft within the arts. Morris's emphasis on nature (fig. 3), his belief in the unity of art and life, and his rejection of a hierarchy in artistic media found a receptive audience among artists in Belgium and France, who incorporated his aesthetic philosophy into the development of the Art Nouveau style.[4]

Like Ruskin and Morris, many Belgian artists were politically liberal and supported progressive causes, including universal suffrage. While they also responded to the negative aspects of industrialization, they were less interested than Ruskin and Morris in creating a social utopia. Their works express not only a desire to break with the past but also an embracing optimism for the new age. Architect Victor Horta, a leading proponent of Art Nouveau in Brussels, designed light-filled, dynamic structures ornamented with bold, undulating curves and soft pastel tones. Another Belgian, Henry van de Velde, left a career in painting for the applied arts. His designs for private residences, furniture, and porcelain drew heavily on plant forms that stretch, bend, and rhythmically undulate. Similarly, the jewelry created in Belgium was based on organic forms, exotic plants, and gossamer insects.

The seminal French Art Nouveau jeweler René Lalique spent two formative years in England during the late 1870s and attended classes at the art school in Sydenham, London, where he was exposed to the writings of Ruskin and the work of Morris. Whereas artists such as Eugène Grasset in France were influenced by Ruskin's Neo-Gothic inclinations when creating their Art Nouveau furniture, ironwork, and architecture, Lalique and his contemporaries in the jewelry world responded to the sensual curves and emphasis on nature found in Morris's designs. But while British Arts and Crafts jewelers preferred the flora of the cultivated garden, for Art Nouveau jewelers nature was most attractive in its uncultivated state, where creeping vines, intoxicating wildflowers, wintry woodlands, and ponds teeming with flying insects dominated the landscape (cat. 60).[5] And while many Arts and Crafts practitioners were trained informally and fabricated their ornaments out of silver, mother-of-pearl, moonstone, and *cloisonné* enamel, Lalique and other Art Nouveau jewelers spent years as apprentices under master jewelers, learning stone setting and the goldsmith's art and becoming highly skilled craftspeople capable of creating jeweled masterworks.

The treatment of nature in the Art Nouveau jewelers' designs also reflects their growing exposure to Japanese art. An intense interest in all things Japanese had swept through Europe and the United States after the opening of Japan to the West in 1854. The passion for Japanese art and decorative handicrafts such as furniture, textiles, metalwork, enamel, lacquer, and porcelain was furthered by Japan's participation in the great international expositions, beginning with the London International Exhibition in 1862. While many of the Japanese objects exhibited at these events were based on tradi-

tional designs, others, such as multisectioned bronze vases with complex scenes, were created for the Western market. Hundreds of thousands of visitors attended the expositions, many of them drawn to the novel forms, sophisticated techniques, and elaborate narratives of these exotic objects;[6] other Japanese crafts were admired for their simple elegance, delicacy, asymmetrical design, and motifs drawn from nature.

Several art dealers, including the German-born Siegfried Bing, were Japan enthusiasts and opened shops featuring Japanese artworks, some of which they acquired while visiting the East. Bing, who was widely respected for his knowledge of Eastern antiquities, became an active member of London's Japan Society in 1892. Shortly afterward, he proposed several close friends for membership, including Henri Vever, an accomplished French jeweler who owned an important collection of Japanese ukiyo-e prints (fig. 4), and P. A. Isaac-Dathis, a Parisian textile designer who incorporated Japanese design elements into his work. By 1895 Bing was advancing the work of these and other artists directly influenced by Japanese art in his newly renovated Paris gallery Maison de l'Art Nouveau.[7] His knowledge, passion, connoisseurship, and extensive contacts in the art world helped establish a global art market for the Art Nouveau style. Most of the artists he featured were European, although several, including Louis Comfort Tiffany, were American.[8] While they represented many different approaches to the new style, they shared a deep appreciation for the flat planes, asymmetry, and celebration of nature found in the arts of Japan.

Bing's gallery space–designed by Henry van de Velde, who was dedicated to the modernization of interior decoration–contained several exhibition galleries that displayed painting, sculpture, and an array of decorative objects for the home. Philosophically, Bing did not distinguish between the fine and applied arts, and the work of several jewelers, including Edward Colonna, Henri Vever, and René Lalique, was displayed in his store. Later, the gallery was expanded to include workshops, one of which was a jewelry design and fabrication studio that had large windows to admit light.[9] Bing's appreciation of jewelry was no doubt influenced by his son Marcel, a noted jeweler who supervised the jewelry workshop and managed his father's business after his death.

Also on display in Bing's galleries were works by the late-nineteenth-century Symbolists, whose avant-garde art had a powerful influence on Art Nouveau. The poets and artists associated with Symbolism challenged the superiority of realism and the scientific objectivism of Impressionism, creating in its place a mystical, subjective reality where emotion and unconscious forces dominated.[10] They were also interested in the process of metamorphosis, creating surreal man-beast hybrids. Art Nouveau jewelers were intrigued by these strange concoctions and created ornaments featuring winged female figures, chimera, and blossoms with human parts (cat. 61). Many of the French Symbolist painters used literary sources as a springboard for their imagination. Their creations have a dreamy, mysterious quality (fig. 5) that Art Nouveau jewelers captured in their miniature works of art (cat. 63). Though not officially a Symbolist, the sculptor Auguste Rodin elicited similarly deep emotions in his works. His techniques of manipulating light and shadow and adding detailed texture to surfaces likewise influenced leaders of the new movement.

Art Nouveau Style

In sharp contrast to the static, naturalistic formulas promulgated by the academies, Art Nouveau artists placed a new emphasis on line that was curved, flowing, exuberant, and sometimes agitated.[11] This graphic innovation formed the aesthetic basis for the bold, linear loops in Victor Horta's private residences; the sinuous, vegetative ironwork in Hector Guimard's Métro stations in Paris; and the graceful, sinuous plant forms in Louis Majorelle's furniture designs (fig. 6).[12] In jewelry, it was most pronounced in the works of French and Belgian artists, whose mastery of the curve resulted in elegant adornments with fluid lines (cat. 22).

Another hallmark of the new style was the symbolic stylization of nature, in which elements of the real world were transformed into iconic images by a process of simplification, abstraction, and harmonization. To this was added a degree of artifice, an attitude derived from the Symbolist movement. According to scholar Paul Greenhalgh, "Many Art Nouveau pattern-forms are a result of nature being coaxed into the realm of artifice. Symbolic conventionalism allowed the poetic imagination to be expressed through natural forms without strictly following the natural world. Unlike previous conventionalist forms, these new shapes might be used to subvert rather than support a sense of stability;

Fig. 6
Louis Majorelle (French, 1859-1926), *Cabinet*, about 1900, various woods, wrought-iron mounts, and silk

they could be used to celebrate individuality, flux or wantonness."[13]

Although the new movement attempted to correct the negative impact of industrialization by substituting one-of-a-kind handcrafted goods for poorly made, mass-produced items, Art Nouveau artists did not oppose technology. They responded to profound social changes such as the introduction of the cinema, the increased pace of transportation, and innovations in long-distance communication with optimism and unbounded energy.[14] Flowing hair, undulating vines, plants at every stage of development, and birds in flight (cat. 44) were but a few of the images that jewelers and other artists used to celebrate the movement, growth, and transformation that characterized the turn of the century. But there was also a darker, edgier side to some of the imagery included in the art, a fin-de-siècle morbidity that was part cultural pessimism and part fear of the approaching modern age. In describing the jewelry of the day, the French novelist Louis-Ferdinand Céline (Destouches) noted, "Everything was

Fig. 7 (opposite)
Victor Horta (Belgian, 1861–1947), *Staircase in the Horta House, rue Americaine, Brussels*, 1898–1901

Fig. 8
Emil Bieber (German, 1878–1962), *René Lalique and his wife Alice*, 1903, carbon print photograph, Musée d'Orsay, Paris

loathsome … The whole crisis of symbolism … Bits of nightmares … Medusas in serpent's knots forming necklaces … More chimeras … Nothing was missing: dragons, demons, sprites, vampires … The insomnias of the whole world."[15] That these unsettling images were so skillfully rendered in precious and exotic materials only added to their appeal.

The stylistic changes in the visual arts that began in France and Belgium quickly spread to other European countries and the Americas. In Glasgow, a city artistically aligned with the Continent, it was manifested in the elegant geometry and simplicity of the architect and designer Charles Rennie Mackintosh. His buildings and interiors, often described as lyrical, emphasized linearized proportions and flat surfaces with stylized floral accents. Additionally, Mackintosh and his circle, known as the Glasgow school, were influenced by a rising nationalism that found expression in the revival of Celtic designs. Like many artists associated with the British Arts and Crafts movement, the Glasgow school aspired to create functional forms within harmonious settings.

In Germany, where an emphasis on naturalism in the decorative arts was replaced by a more abstract, geometric style, the new movement was known as Jugendstil (Youth Style), a name derived from the Munich-based magazine *Jugend*. Otto Eckmann, a contributor to the publication and a proponent of the new style, abandoned painting for a career in design. His work, characterized by rhythmic, curvilinear plant forms, is a blend of the abstract and the naturalistic. The same fusion of styles is evident in the decorative objects and jewelry made in the Munich area, including the work of jeweler Karl Rothmüller (cat. 26). In nearby Austria, a geometric linearism dominated the arts. Architects Josef Hoffmann and Josef Olbrich led the movement, emphasizing line that was rectilinear rather than sinuous (fig. 9). The jewelry created by Hoffmann and other Vienna Secessionists was truly avant-garde, anticipating abstraction and nonobjective art.

Art Nouveau in Spain was centered in Barcelona. At the close of the nineteenth century, the city had experienced unprecedented growth, becoming the country's leading industrial center. Political, cultural, and economic reforms transformed the area, as did the Moorish-inspired *modernista* architecture of Antoni Gaudí. Dramatic, daring, and emotionally charged, his spectacular buildings were lavishly ornamented with colorful tiles arranged in rhythmic repetitions. Serpentine patterns and arabesques also dominated the jewelry created by Catalan jewelers, including the firm Fuset Grau (cat. 30).

The Art Nouveau style that was adopted in the United States was less flamboyant, smaller in scale, and often combined with other contemporary trends, so that it was not uncommon for a single piece to exhibit features common to the revivalist, Arts and Crafts, and Art Nouveau movements (cat. 78).[16] The work of Louis Comfort Tiffany, the artist most closely identified with the movement, demonstrates this eclecticism. Even artist-jewelers strongly identified with the American Arts and Crafts tradition, such as Frank Gardner Hale (cat. 32), were not immune to the allure of Art Nouveau's graceful curves and elegant asymmetries.

Materials and Techniques

Art Nouveau jewelers chose materials for their aesthetic properties rather than their intrinsic worth. This was a radical departure from the prior two centuries, when precious metals and gemstones were the substances of choice. During that period, the diamond was held in high regard, and jewelry was designed specifically to display this costly gem to best advantage. Art Nouveau artists, in contrast, used the diamond sparingly, adding sparkle and highlights to areas awash in colored enamel.[17] An example is Georges Fouquet's orchid brooch (cat. 20), in which the pale pastel coloration of the enamel softly shimmers with tiny bezel-set diamonds reminiscent of early-morning dew. Similarly, in his brooch with leaves and blossoms (cat. 21), Fouquet employed small, glistening diamonds along the edge of the golden frame. Both of these jewels use extraordinary baroque pearls whose color (in the case of the orchid) and asymmetrical shape (in the floral brooch) were selected to enhance the overall design. Unlike the perfectly round and color-matched strands of natural pearls worn by well-to-do women in Europe and the United States during the nineteenth century, irregularly shaped pearls, often used as drops in Art Nouveau pendants (cat. 67), were considerably less costly and often more compelling visually. In a fringe necklace with blister pearls by Lalique (cat. 10), the trio of luminous pearls on each pendant is accentuated by the pale green iridescence of the surrounding enamel. It is the design and color harmonies that breathe life into these modest gems.

As for colored gemstones, Art Nouveau

Fig. 9
Josef Hoffmann (Austrian, 1870–1956), *Teapot*, 1904, silver, ebony, and raffia

jewelers used them in a manner reminiscent of a painter drawing on an extensive color palette. For example, the faceted pink sapphire pendant in Lalique's pendant-brooch with pink carnations (cat. 2) augments the muted color of the frosted glass blossoms, while the high polish of the stone contrasts with the soft, silky surface of the petals. Artists also used colored gems to intensify contour lines, as evidenced in the row of channel-set rubies outlining the bottom edge of the upper wings in Philippe Wolfers' *Dragonfly* pendant-brooch (cat. 38). The ingenious coloration of the enamel on the insect's lower wings, which shifts from deep pink to pale green, complements the gem-studded tips of the upper wings. That the ethereal, transparent wings of the moth are not burdened by the density and weight of the stones has much to do with the masterly use of tint and shade.

Of all the gemstones used by Art Nouveau jewelers, the most popular was the opal, a fragile stone with a range of iridescence and fire. Some of the most extraordinary specimens were obtained from Australia, where opal was first mined in the 1870s. Lalique was attracted to boulder opal, a form of the gem that includes part of the host ironstone rock. When boulder opal was used, the matrix of the gem formed an integral part of the design (cat. 36). Opal was also carved as cabochon stones (cat. 1), in thin sheets for landscape backgrounds, in small squares set as a mosaic (cat. 70), and as figural parts in representations of plants and animals.

In contrast to the all-white look characteristic of late-nineteenth-century jewelry, Art Nouveau artists worked primarily in yellow gold, occasionally highlighting it with small

diamonds set in platinum (cat. 23).[18] For color, they relied primarily on enamel, a vitreous material composed of powdered silica, potash, and metallic oxide colorants. When these ingredients are mixed, applied to a metal substrate, and then heated, a glassy, colorful surface is formed. Some enamel techniques, such as *cloisonné* and *champlevé*, have been known since antiquity, while others, including *plique à jour* enamel, became fashionable during the late nineteenth century.[19] *Plique à jour* is backless, which allows light to pass through a network of cells filled with translucent enamel, resulting in a dramatic, stained-glass effect. It can be particularly stunning in three-dimensional works such as hair ornaments, and was masterfully employed by Art Nouveau jewelers to fabricate blossoms, winged insects, and other aspects of the natural world (cat. 20). *Cabochonné* enameling, a variant of *plique à jour*, was also used to great effect at the turn of the century. In this case, layers of transparent enamel are built up in imitation of cabochons, unfaceted stones polished into a convex form. Comte Enguerrand du Suau de la Croix, a master of *cabochonné*, used this gemlike technique in both jewelry and decorative arts objects (cat. 69).

Art Nouveau artists also used nontraditional materials in their ornaments. An example is horn, which ranges in color from ebony to cream and when subjected to heat and pressure can become translucent or transparent. Although horn was used for utilitarian and decorative objects from antiquity onward, the material gradually disappeared from use with the arrival of man-made, moldable plastics in the late nineteenth century. However, several

Fig. 10
Emile Gallé (French, 1846–1904), *Vase*, 1891, cased and carved glass

artists in late-nineteenth-century France, including René Lalique, Louis Aucoc, and Lucien Gaillard, were attracted to the material, which they heated, molded, carved, dyed, and inlaid with gemstones and colored enamels. First used by Lalique in the mid-1890s, horn was especially suitable for the wings of dragon-flies and moths (cat. 42), adding a delicate airi-ness to these diaphanous structures.[20] It was also used for the tooth component of hair ornaments.

Elephant ivory was another organic mater-ial used by Lalique and other Art Nouveau jew-elers, partly because of its availability. When Leopold II of Belgium managed to gain control of the Congo in 1885, he laid claim to the region's rich natural resources, one of which was ivory.[21] The jewelers selected this soft, creamy substance to create low-relief scenes, the heads of dreamy-faced women, the petals of carved blossoms, and a variety of hair ornaments (cat. 9).

Lalique was also regarded as an exceptional innovator in glass. In his earliest experiments with this medium, he molded three-dimensional glass blossoms in soft pastel shades that were incorporated into larger constructions made of gold, enamel, and gemstones (cat. 8). Later, he adapted the *pâte de verre* glassmaking tech-nique to jewelry, using powdered glass that was fired in a mold and then lightly enameled (cat. 55).[22] In other ornaments, entire landscapes were made of molded glass, whose surface finish ranged from a soft matte to a shimmering gloss.

While Lalique and his contemporaries were forward-looking in their choice of materials, they were not averse to working with materials used in historic adornments. One unusual example is Lalique's flowering tree brooch (cat. 13), which has a distinctly Japanesque flavor. The selection of steel for this brooch, created relatively late in Lalique's jewelry career, may have been inspired by mid-nineteenth-century iron and steel ornaments in the Rocco and Neoclassical styles.[23] The motif, however, clearly conveys the artist's affinity for the East (fig. 11).

From a technical point of view, Art Nouveau jewelry represents the most innovative and sophisticated jewelry ever created. The ornaments are also stunningly beautiful, and it is often noted that the jewelry is as striking on the reverse as it is on the front (cat. 44). For many, these jewels are more objets d'art than adornments, and they were collected during their time for display rather than wear. As for the legacy of the new style, the studio jewelry movement that emerged during the 1940s and 1950s in the United States and Europe empha-sized good design over traditional, precious materials; unique, one-of-a-kind handcrafted ornaments; and technical innovation. It is the spirit of Art Nouveau that continues to inspire collectors and craftspeople.

Fig. 11
Araki Tomei (Japanese,
1817–1870), *Pair of menuki*,
mid–late 19th century, gold

SYMBOLS AND MOTIFS IN ART NOUVEAU JEWELRY

Elyse Zorn Karlin

It is striking how well the motifs on most Art Nouveau jewelry fall into several subject categories. Responding to a range of influences including Symbolism, Japanese art, the Rococo, religious currents, scientific developments, and shifting gender roles, the movement's jewelry artists adopted a specific set of recurring motifs–primarily, sinuously curving lines, aspects of nature, and the eroticized female form–that expressed particular meanings and shared sensibilities.

Their use of motifs as symbols derived in part from the Symbolist movement, one of the most important influences on Art Nouveau. Symbolism had adherents throughout Europe and–to a limited extent–in the United States, first in literature and then in fine art and music. The movement's manifesto, written in 1886 by the Greek poet, essayist, and art critic Jean Moréas, announced that Symbolism was hostile to "plain meanings, declamations, false sentimentality and matter-of-fact description" and that its aim was to "clothe the Ideal in a perceptible form" whose "goal was not in itself, but whose sole purpose was to express the Ideal."[1] Affiliated writers and artists used symbols to represent ideas, choosing words, forms, and colors that would deliver their personal messages about spiritual, moral, religious, and political matters–but with deliberate ambiguity and hermetism.

If the iconography found in Art Nouveau jewelry were strictly of the Symbolist genre, it would offer a veiled and mysterious message understood by only a small circle of people close to the artistan, as was the Symbolists writers' and painters' intent. But clearly this is not the case. Art Nouveau jewelers adopted the spirit of Symbolism without its esotericism. Repeated motifs appear in the work of many jewelers of the era, as well as within the oeuvre of a single jeweler. By virtue of their ubiquity, these specific icons become less mysterious, although their meanings are often complex; unlike the motifs used by the Symbolists, they stood for something that was meant to be recognized and appreciated by those with artistic tastes and sensibilities.

Art Nouveau jewelers, like the designers of the movement's architecture and domestic items, drew their motifs from a number of sources, interpreting and combining them in unique ways. For example, in France, artists were inspired by eighteenth-century design, Japanese art, and the artwork of other cultures considered exotic, such as Islamic and Egyptian designs. In Dutch Art Nouveau, the influence of the Indonesian colonies and batik art blended with motifs from nature. Danish *skonvirke* jewelry combined Scandinavian symbols with designs borrowed from both French Art Nouveau and English Arts and Crafts. Traditional Celtic motifs were featured in the Irish art jewelry of the period. The unifying thread for the jewelry artists in all countries was that they attempted not to reject the past but rather to mold it like a piece of clay into something new and exciting. No matter which motifs they interpreted, the objects they crafted were often steeped in fantasy. If a familiar symbol was selected, it was often

fused with some other motif or cultural influence to make the end result something exotic–such as a woman with butterfly wings and delicate antennae extending from her forehead.

Such fantasies sprang, of course, from the fertile minds of the jewelry artists, but they were also generated by the cultural climate of the time. Members of the avant-garde in many countries were intoxicated with new ways of thinking at the turn of the twentieth century and were inspired by those with imagination. This was an age of experimentation–not unlike the 1960s and the so-called Age of Aquarius. Some artistic circles were investigating alternative forms of religion, such as Rosicrucianism, which was founded on a belief in the occult arts, and Theosophy, a religious philosophy that states all religions are attempts to approach the absolute and that there is some portion of truth in each.[2] Several artisans created jewelry based on Theosophical motifs, using certain colors to represent various hierarchies of spiritualism. Many people were interested in the mystical, and séances were in vogue.[3] Even Satanism attracted followers.

As is often the case at the end of a century, exaggerated predictions and psychological investigations abounded, as thinkers considered new ways of looking at the individual's place in society. The field of formal psychology was in its infancy, and Sigmund Freud was promoting his controversial theories of the unconscious mind. His ideas about the mechanism of repression, the directing of sexual desire toward a variety of objects, and the importance of dreams as a source of insight into unconscious yearnings created quite a stir as the century emerged from its

Victorian primness. Freud encouraged a "cult of self" that became popular in literary and artistic circles in Europe and the United States.

Writers, artists, and musicians of the Symbolist movement, who would influence Art Nouveau designers, devised their own theories about how to access one's individual psyche, especially the dream state. They experimented with hypnotism, hallucination induced by psychotropic drugs, and other means of exploring the unconscious and heightening their senses. They were not the first artists to exploit the effects of mind-altering drugs, but their use of them was widespread. Absinthe was commonly consumed, since many artists believed that the hallucinations brought on by "the green muse" aided their creativity. In Bohemian circles in Paris and London, artists drank large quantities of the potent liqueur, both by itself and combined with other alcoholic beverages or recreational drugs. Opium was also readily available from India, an English colony.

The Symbolist artworks that arose from these psychogenic investigations mixed myths and imagery culled from the dream state, represented by iconic representations that were personally meaningful to the artist but not necessarily understood by the general public. Fernand Khnopff's *The Caress*, for instance, depicts a bare-chested man being stroked by a creature with a woman's head and a leopard's body. Only the artist and perhaps those closest to him were meant to understand the significance of this fantasy. Posters, paintings, jewelry, and metalwork produced by Margaret and Frances MacDonald and their circle in Scotland, who became known as the "spook school," featured

Fig. 12 (detail)
Léon Nikolaievitch Bakst
(Russian, 1866–1924), *The Butterfly (costume design for Anna Pavlova)*, 1913, watercolor and graphite pencil on paper

ghostly elongated and otherworldly female figures, as did the graphic art of Jan Toorop in the
Netherlands (fig. 13). In music of the period,
composers such as Claude Debussy were influenced by the Symbolist writers. Debussy's best-
known work, *Prélude à l'après-midi d'un faune*
(Prelude to the Afternoon of a Faun), is based
on a poem by the Symbolist poet Stéphane
Mallarmé. When performed as a ballet, it features a solo dancer rising from sleep to move
in a languid manner and then returning to his
dreams. All of these imaginative artistic and
intellectual endeavors contributed to an atmos-
phere that stimulated the creation of jewelry
designs with shared motifs that were unprece-
dentedly inventive and fantastic.

The "Whiplash" Line

Each of the "new art" movements that emerged
about 1900 was somehow related to a sense of
nationalism. In France, where Art Nouveau
reached its zenith, several events contributed
to the development of that style. Following its
defeat in the Franco-Prussian War in 1871,
France was forced to come to grips with its
decreasing status as a world power. Additionally, two scandals rocked the nation: government corruption involving the building of the
Panama Canal and the Dreyfus Affair–the
wrongful conviction of a Jewish artillery offi-
cer, which drove a deep wedge between two ide-
ological sides and led to a rise in anti-Semitism.
Further public anxiety resulted from the strug-
gle over Roman Catholicism's dominance as
the state religion. Beginning in 1880, one of the
goals of the new republican government was to
promote the secular values established by the

French Revolution, and in 1905 the church and
state were finally separated.

The convergence of these difficult events
created a longing among the French for their
country's most glorious period, the eighteenth
century, a time when Paris was the leading
trendsetter in the arts. The government under-
took the renovation of the Palace of Versailles
(the center of power in ancien-régime France)
and the Rococo core of the Bibliothèque
nationale, and for the first time the Louvre set
aside a gallery to display eighteenth-century
furniture and decorative items. It is in the
curved and sinuous lines of Rococo architecture and decorative arts that Art Nouveau
artists found a prime ingredient of their style:
the "whiplash," or undulating line, which is
especially prevalent in jewels, architecture, and
graphic arts. Additional connections between
the two design movements include a fascination
with the exotic East, an emphasis on asymmetry
(cat. 29), a focus on the beauty of nature in fan-
tasized form, and the use of organic shapes.[4]

Art Nouveau not only revived these inter-
ests but took them to an extreme. A typically
Rococo ewer made in Toulouse in 1763 (fig. 14),
for instance, features a large scroll handle with
chased leaf decorations and a scrolling leaf as
the thumbpiece. René Lalique isolated and
exaggerated these elements in his hair comb
decorated with ivy leaves (cat. 5). The sensuous
curve of the ewer's handle is the precursor to
the gold and enamel spiral of the hair comb,
and the use of nature as decoration is vital to
both pieces. But in Lalique's ornament, the
scrolls and the leaves become the very essence
of the object.

Fig. 13
Jan Toorop (Dutch, 1858–
1929), *Delftsche Slaolie*
(Delft Salad Oil), 1894,
lithographic poster in color

By referencing the Rococo in Art Nouveau design, artists aimed to return French art to prominence. Both movements were reactions to the excess of the styles that immediately preceded them. The Rococo developed in response to the overly ornamented decoration, emotionally charged drama, and often overtly religious subject matter of the earlier Baroque period: as Louis xiv's reign came to an end, weighty Baroque designs gave way to more delicate forms with lighter elements, plentiful curves, and naturalistic patterns. Similarly, Art Nouveau was a response to the fussiness of nineteenth-century Victorian design, which emphasized excessive ornamentation, heavy fabrics, overstuffed furniture, and too much of everything. This visual cacophony was partly motivated by members of the nouveau-riche class that had emerged during the Industrial Revolution, who wanted to show off what they could afford by cramming their homes to excess. Motivated by a desire to refocus and reinvigorate the decorative arts, the Art Nouveau style, with its characteristic undulating line, exhibits a lightness and openness that stand in stark contrast to the heaviness of Victorian design.

Nature

Nature is one of the most pervasive themes depicted on Art Nouveau jewelry, often in combination with the human figure. This interest was not new: throughout the eighteenth and nineteenth centuries, images from the natural world were at the forefront of jewelry design. The naturalistically styled diamond jewelry of the Georgian period (1714–1837) was cleverly set with springs so that it would sway each time

the wearer moved (an effect called *en tremblant*), as if a gentle breeze was blowing the petals of a flower resting on a woman's bosom. And in the Victorian period (1837–1901), a "language of flowers" developed in which specific flowers represented particular sentiments. There even existed briefly, at the height of the Victorian period, an odd fad for mounting hummingbird heads and iridescent Brazilian beetles onto jewelry. A number of factors contributed to the ongoing fascination with nature. Artists were inspired by scientific studies of flora and fauna, and the publication of Charles Darwin's *Origin of Species* in 1859 sparked an interest in evolution. Designers in Great Britain and the rest of Europe were also influenced by the nineteenth-century writings of John Ruskin and William Morris, both of whom advocated that nature should be the basis for all art.

Several art jewelry movements turned to nature as a predominant theme at the turn of the twentieth century, but each expressed the interest quite differently. For example, British Arts and Crafts jewelers depicted nature in a realistic and straightforward manner. A Limoges enamel inset in a belt buckle (fig. 15) designed by the well-known English Arts and Crafts jewelers Edith and Nelson Dawson features the motif of a single blossom of a reddish pink flower, mounted in a *repoussé* silver plaque ornamented with turquoise cabochons. Self-taught in enameling, the Dawsons did not have the technical expertise of the highly skilled French Art Nouveau jewelers. Their thick, dense enamel offers a stylistic but recognizable depiction of a flower (possibly a carnation) that is solid and unmoving, failing to capture its inherent sensuality.

Contemporary Art Nouveau jewelers, in contrast, incorporated all aspects of nature, both real and mythical, and vibrantly brought them to life with undulating planes, shimmering enamels, and fluid lines. René Lalique's carnation brooch (cat. 1), made of gold,

Fig. 14 (opposite)
Louis Samson II (French),
Covered ewer, 1763, silver

Fig. 15
Nelson Dawson (English, 1859–1942) and Edith Dawson (English), *Arts and Crafts waist ornament*, about 1905, silver, enamel, and turquoise

enamel, opal, and glass, is a far more vibrant and sensual depiction of a flower than the Dawsons'. The delicate and complicated *plique à jour* enamel, illuminated by light passing through it, differs markedly from the deep enamel and dark blue background of the Dawson belt. Whereas the Dawsons' flower is charmingly naive, almost as if portrayed by a child, the Lalique carnation presents an adult's complicated fantasy, a glimpse of nature charged with sexuality and excitement. And while the small Dawson enamel is executed within the confines of a circle, the Lalique brooch follows the natural curves of the flower, offering an image that seems to spring directly from nature.

As the leading jeweler of his time, Lalique set the bar for the exquisite portrayal of nature in jewelry. His magnificent designs addressed the changing of the seasons and other rhythms of nature, and his motifs encompassed creatures of both the day and the night, with a special affinity for bats and owls. Typical of Art Nouveau jewels, his flowers, birds, animals, and insects could appear either beautiful and ethereal or grotesque and frightening. Lalique drew his inspiration from the rural setting of Ay, in Champagne, where he was born, spent summer holidays, and returned throughout his life. As an avid photographer, he saw nature through his camera lens, a habit that partly explains the realistic qualities of his jewelry designs. However, he generally did not portray the most pleasing cycles of nature, preferring to show a bare tree trunk or a pine branch rather than a full green tree at the height of summer. Whereas in Arts and Crafts jewelry

nature was illustrated at its best–for instance, a flower in full bloom–in Art Nouveau ornaments it was shown in all of its phases: from a plant's first bloom (cat. 8) to its withering and eventual demise, or an insect's evolution through metamorphosis.

The natural motifs that appear in the designs of Lalique and his contemporaries, who included Georges Fouquet, Louis Aucoc, Lucien Falize, Eugène Feuillâtre, and Lucien Gaillard, also indicate the strong influence of Japanese art. Many artists of this period felt that the relationship between nature and design had been lost, and they looked to Japanese art–in which nature played a critical role–to aid them in rekindling it. Landscapes, especially waterscapes, were a frequent theme in jewelry, and a number of Lalique's landscapes of water– whether a still lake or a flowing waterfall–are reminiscent of scenes in Japanese woodcuts, both in their simplistic form and in their coloration. He was also fond of underwater inhabitants such as fish, sea horses, and seaweed, many of which are featured in Japanese woodcuts.

Lalique's depictions of trees and flowers likewise drew on Japanese images. One steel brooch (cat. 13; steel, incidentally, was an unusual material to use in jewelry at that time) shows a tree branch heavily laden with blossoms, its bent limbs curving in an interlacing design. A similar arc can be seen in the trees in the print *View of Matsuchiyama*, designed by the artist Utagawa Hiroshige I during the Edo period (fig. 16). Just as the trees are the most prominent element in the woodcut, making the distant cityscape secondary to the composition,

東都名所
真乳山
之図

the unpolished-steel branch dominates Lalique's jewel; the only background is a lower level of steel that is polished to create a contrasting, three-dimensional effect similar to the relationship between Hiroshige's foreground and background.

Of the wide variety of flowers that adorn Art Nouveau jewels—poppies, carnations, morning glories, sweet peas, roses, bleeding hearts, cherry blossoms, and irises—at least the latter two derive from Asian art. Other plant materials depicted include thistles, pinecones, ivy, seaweed, bamboo, and berries. The leaf of the ginkgo plant, which has been used in family crests in Japan since the Middle Ages, appears frequently in these ornaments, as well as in the jewelry and decorative objects of the American Arts and Crafts movement. As is often the case

Fig. 16
Utagawa Hiroshige I (Japanese, 1797-1858), *View of Matsuchiyama*, from the series *Famous Places in the Eastern Capital*, about 1840-42, woodblock print

with Asian symbols, the ginkgo leaf has multiple meanings: peace, longevity, life and death, hope, love, East and West, yin and yang. By far the most important and sensual of the flora rendered into jewelry was the orchid, one of the most breathtaking of subjects (cat. 20). The French Art Nouveau glassmaker Emile Gallé described this exotic flower as having "richness, an inconceivable strangeness of forms, species, odours, colourations, whims, voluptuousness and unsettling mysteries."[5]

Lalique and other Art Nouveau jewelers borrowed images of butterflies and other insects from Japanese art as well. The butterflies, bees, grasshoppers, moths, and dragonflies that frequently appear on their jewels (cat. 40) are often fabricated with the most exquisite *plique à jour* enamel, a material that emulated the transparent features of an insect's wing. In fact, the rediscovery of *plique à jour* in the late nineteenth century partly suggested these subjects to the jewelers. Light could pass through this type of enamel and give delicate and diaphanous outstretched wings a glow not possible with *cloisonné* or *champlevé* enamel. Such fabulous insect creations do not appear in the works of Arts and Crafts jewelers, only a handful of whom employed *plique à jour* enameling, but they abound in Art Nouveau jewelry, for which the *plique à jour* technique became a cornerstone.

In addition to insects, snakes are prevalent in Art Nouveau jewelry, especially in pieces by Lalique. The serpent is a symbol of both life and sexuality, and numerous legends connect gemstones with snakes. One story tells that in the temples of Apollo in ancient Greece, where serpents were considered sacred, amber was placed with them as a sign of respect; as a result, amber became associated with snakes, and it was said that each gave power to the other. Lalique's earliest jewels centering on the snake were commissions for the famed actress Sarah Bernhardt. He also designed jewels with snake forms for his important patron Calouste Gulbenkian, an Armenian businessman. Lalique's snakes were most often wrapped around a woman's head or body, the imagery of the serpent both conceptually and physically wound up in his vision of women. This association may have a number of mythological references: Eve in the Garden of Eden, seduced by the snake into eating the forbidden apple; Medusa, with her hair of snakes, whose eyes turned men into stone; or Cleopatra, the Egyptian queen who took a poisonous asp upon her breast to commit suicide rather than become a trophy of Rome. As a decorative motif, the snake was the embodiment of the sinuous line that is at the heart of Art Nouveau design. It was simultaneously pleasing, as it twisted and meandered sensuously, and frightening in its association with danger and the erotic.

Such paradoxical connotations are common in Art Nouveau design.

Fig. 17 (opposite)
Alphonse Mucha (Czechoslovakian, 1860–1939), *Art Nouveau–style vestibule from the Fouquet jewelry shop*, 1900–1910

Fig. 18
Yoshioka Inabanosuke (Japanese), *Tsuba with design of peacock*, 18th century, *shakudō*, gold, and copper

The movement was complex and diverse, and different artists blended its many influences into wildly varying interpretations that depended in part on where they lived and what their personal beliefs and tastes were. The marriage of Rococo sensibilities to Japanese art and Symbolist fantasy led to the embrace of seemingly contradictory tendencies–glorifying the golden age of Rococo France while also exhibiting a fascination with decadent sensuality and death. This latter penchant is exemplified by the imagery of the nightmare–the dark world of the night–that appears as one facet of the dream state in Art Nouveau jewelry. Bats, owls, and other nocturnal creatures are frequent subjects of the ornaments. Although a symbol of good luck and longevity in Asian history, in Western culture the bat is associated with the menacing darkness that descends with the setting of the sun. Bats are also linked with vampires and are therefore another aspect of the late-nineteenth-century interest in the occult. In Art Nouveau jewelry, the bat is a sinister creature: his eyes stare out in a foreboding manner, and his outstretched arms threaten to swoop down and attack. Vultures and eagles, with *plique à jour* wings, could be portrayed as equally frightening.

Like earlier jewelry artists, Art Nouveau designers rendered many identifiable types of birds on their ornaments. Some of the loveliest creations of the Victorian era were brooches of diamonds set in silver depicting groups of swallows or other birds in flight. Art Nouveau jewelers depicted not only swallows, vultures, and eagles but also swans, roosters, and cockerels. Perhaps most characteristic of the period was the peacock–also a popular Victorian symbol and a common image in Japanese art (fig. 18). Various cultures have considered the peacock motif a protection against the evil eye, a symbol of resurrection, or an emblem of pride. The exotic bird makes an appearance in all of the art jewelry movements at the end of the nineteenth century, as well as on textiles and decorative arts in Art Nouveau and on English and American Arts and Crafts objects. Louis Comfort Tiffany, the leading American exponent of art jewelry, was so fond of peacocks that he once held a dinner in which his daughters wore elaborate peacock headdresses while serving the bird as part of the meal.[6] For Art Nouveau artists, the peacock represented a combination of two aspects of nature–beauty and fantasy. Their use of the motif in jewelry is most likely also a historical reference to many cultures for which the peacock's tail represents the sun and moon–darkness and light–a popular theme in Art Nouveau.[7] Artisans often adorned their peacock designs with enamel, adding moonstones and opals for their translucent quality and blue-green coloration (cat. 45).

Although birds, insects, and plants are the subject of Art Nouveau jewels far more often than four-legged beasts, the animal kingdom is occasionally represented. No explanations have yet been offered for the meaning of these motifs, but the wide range of creatures depicted is worth noting. Domestic sheep and cows sometimes make an appearance, as do fantasy creatures including dragons, chimera, and griffins. Less common are beasts of the wild such as lions and panthers. Magical beings were not confined to the animal world; fantastical human forms are also seen–among them, mermaids, wood nymphs, and fairies (cat. 66).

Women and the Erotic

After nature, the representation of women is the most frequent theme in Art Nouveau jewelry. Previously in France, the use of even a woman's face on jewelry was considered distasteful, but with the arrival of the new style, far more than just her face was displayed.[8] Women were portrayed in many different ways: a head in full face or profile, with long flowing tresses that stretch and curl (cat. 62); a half-woman, half-insect hybrid; a full-bodied figure either unclothed or dressed in a swirling gossamer fabric (cat. 67). The historical cultures that Art Nouveau jewelers looked to offered subjects with erotic overtones, such as the woman as a siren or the Sphinx. One forbidding type was a Medusa-like creature with snakes writhing around her head. Other characterizations ranged from mildly coquettish to downright erotic, from chaste and dreamy to evil temptress or femme fatale.

These widely varied representations manifest the conflicting feelings that different segments of society harbored toward women and their changing role in society. The liberated "new woman" who was emerging at the end of the nineteenth century was both celebrated and feared. The majority of French men were reluctant to see women get an education or a job, since those endeavors took them out of the home and threatened the unity of the family, or so they thought. Government officials were especially concerned because France's birthrate was declining. They reasoned that women who had careers or attended school were less likely to be at home having babies. Many writers of the time, including the brothers Edmond and Jules de Goncourt and Octave Uzanne, expounded on this "problem" of the *femme nouvelle*, advising young men to avoid marrying women looking for a life outside their domestic role.

In discussions of culture, these writers claimed that women should be associated with the decorative arts, since that branch of art involved decorating the domestic realm. These men had no objection to women's being artistic as long as they did not leave the home to use their talents. In addition, they argued that the female form was a fitting motif for decorative objects—that it was, in fact, essential to the vitality of the French decorative arts. Their theories influenced the government officials responsible for reviving French craft, who united with them to celebrate the woman who knew her place and stayed in the home caring for her family. We see evidence of this effort in the government's commission of new coinage. When Oscar Roty, an important designer of medals in the Art Nouveau style, was chosen to design coins in the new series, he broke with the past in his depiction of Marianne, the traditional symbol of France. Whereas previous artists had always represented Marianne as a matronly figure, Roty portrayed her as a young, agile, and barefoot woman wearing long flowing robes, with her hair waving freely behind her. This new symbol of French womanhood was the antithesis of the *femme nouvelle*, who wore bloomers, rode bicycles, smoked cigarettes, and agitated for the right to vote. Roty's provocative depiction promoted the traditional domestic role, subjugating women by defining them as sexual objects.

In general, men in contemporary artistic and Bohemian circles supported the women's movement. There is evidence that English Arts and Crafts jewelers sympathized with the suffragist movement, and many women artists achieved fame in English and American Arts and Crafts jewelry. The leanings of the Art Nouveau artists, however, are less clear. Interestingly, not a single female Art Nouveau jeweler's name is well known today, although there were a few women designers within the movement. And while Lalique, Alphonse Mucha, and other male artists were patronized by strong women such as the actresses Sarah Bernhardt and Eleanor Duse, the portrayals of women in their jewelry, with flowing hair, long robes, and delicate bodies, are clearly related to the new Marianne of the official coinage. On the one hand, these depictions returned women to a managed role in which they were glorified as sexual objects. But on the other hand, the sensual images conveyed a sense of freedom that reflected a contrasting, and equally current, characterization. The American dancer Loïe Fuller became famous in Paris at this time for performing in silky clothing outfitted with rods that allowed the newly invented electric lights to shine through the fabric as she moved. Her dancing mesmerized watchers, as she appeared to literally undergo a metamorphosis—changing into a new woman in a new century. The Art Nouveau designs can likewise be seen to celebrate the bursting forth of a new kind of woman. Jewelers often joined the female face and figure with plant tendrils or dragonflies' wings, connecting women with nature (cat. 72). This iconography simultaneously suggests "ideal" female beauty, sensual energy, and fear of the femme fatale.

The Art Nouveau artists' complicated portrayal of women was also affected by their exposure to Japanese art, which must have included knowledge of the erotic representation of female figures in netsuke carvings (toggles used to secure a small container suspended from the sash of a kimono) and *shunga* prints (erotic woodblock prints that depict scenes from the Yoshiwara, a brothel section of the city of Edo that had its own moral codes for behavior). The octopus—which has erotic significance in *shunga* prints—sometimes shows up in Art Nouveau ornaments. In addition, jewelers would have been familiar with the Japanese cultural phenomenon of geisha girls, women whose job it was to be traditionally feminine and to entertain men with their performances of dancing and music.

Turn-of-the-century Europe was the time of the demimonde, women such as Liane de Pougy and Cléo de Mérode who made their fortunes as courtesans to important men. These women were both submissive to men and independent enough to look out for themselves.[9] They tended to perform in the theater—either as actresses or as dancers—occupations that brought them fame and wealth, and they used their sexuality to create their stage personas. Perhaps the best-known example is Sarah Bernhardt, who also dabbled in sculpture. Self-aware of the power she possessed as a demimonde, Bernhardt fashioned a bronze inkwell into a mysterious self-portrait as a sphinx, with the body of a griffin, wings of a bat, and tail of a fish–a rich example of the use of mythical creatures in Art Nouveau metalwork and a metaphor for the actress's ability to transform herself, both onstage and off (fig. 19). Two of the most famous Art Nouveau jewelers–René Lalique and Alphonse Mucha–designed jewelry for Bernhardt, and Mucha also executed fabulous posters of the Divine Sarah (fig. 20).

Ambiguous depictions of women appeared in other art of the time as well. During this period at least two well-known painters executed works known as *The Vampire*. The Norwegian Symbolist painter Edvard Munch created his painting in 1894. This work shows a woman wrapping herself around a man and has variously been interpreted as the blood-sucking act of a vampire or simply a sensual embrace. Only a few years later, the British artist Philip Burne-Jones (son of the Pre-Rapaelite painter Edward Burne-Jones) exhibited his most famous work, also known as *The Vampire* (1897), which depicts a woman leaning over a man who lies seemingly comatose on a bed. Both artists had experienced tragic love affairs, which may have influenced their respective images. Each image casts a woman in a dual role–desirable and sexual, but also overpowering. The dichotomy presented in Art Nouveau jewelry is the same: depending on the artist's and the viewer's leanings, a naked woman (a frequent motif) might be perceived as vulnerably objectified or seductively powerful; a woman depicted as Medusa or Salome embodied self-reliance and terrible beauty, sexual appeal and the threat of dominance. While many at the time saw the word

erotic as a synonym for *modern*, others saw eroticism as dangerous.

The Art Nouveau style, in jewelry and in other genres, held sway for a relatively brief time–approximately fifteen years. Some say its demise was brought on by a blatant eroticism that was not acceptable to the mainstream public, but its end was probably due to a combination of factors. Art Nouveau ornaments were not for everyone–they were meant for the rich and the artistic, not for the bourgeoisie. In addition, they were not always that wearable. The use of *plique à jour* enamel, which set Art Nouveau apart from other jewelry, also made the ornaments so delicate that they would break easily: one fall could quickly destroy the enamel of an expensive jewel. Some of Lalique's jewels were so large and cumbersome that women bought them as status symbols but did not wear them; these elaborate pieces sat in jewel boxes as objects to be adored but not worn. And Lalique himself, the leader in creating Art Nouveau jewelry, abandoned the genre for glassmaking in 1914, about the same time that World War I turned life upside down in the countries where Art Nouveau flourished. Last, clothing styles changed at the beginning of the twentieth century. The exquisite brooch of a naked woman-insect, lithe and curving, that exemplified Art Nouveau had no place on the white lace dresses that became popular during the Edwardian period (1900-1910); these gowns were worn with platinum and diamond jewelry that imitated the lace, demonstrating what the public approved of as appropriate attire for women.

Although the production of Art Nouveau jewels lasted only a decade and a half, today

these ornaments represent a great moment in the history of the decorative arts. The artists who created them converted their fantasies into jewels imbued with meaning and turned ordinary materials into objects of incredible sensuality. Part of the style's appeal was its dualism. It was at once a revivalist movement and something new. It simultaneously cele-brated women and epitomized the fear of them. It depicted both the beautiful and the darker sides of nature. Sometimes the orna-ments were so realistic they were surreal, and other times so fantastic they dazzled. Always, they drew the viewer into their exotic world with an emotional power that jewelry rarely possesses.

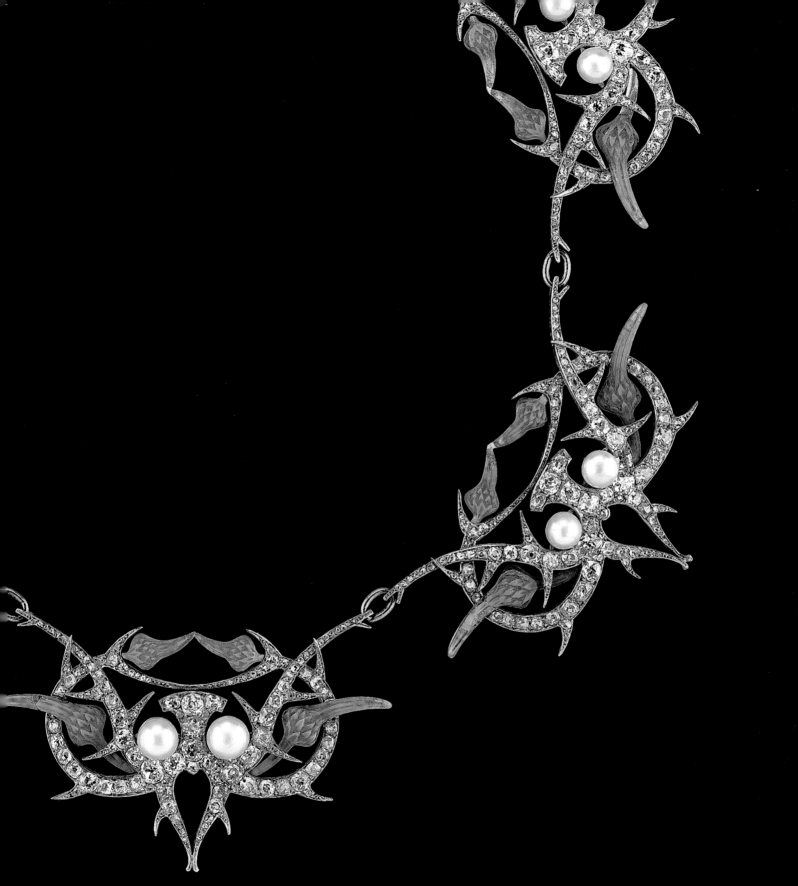

Flora

I
RENÉ LALIQUE
French, 1860–1945
Carnation brooch,
1900–1902
Gold, enamel, opal, and
cast glass

2
RENÉ LALIQUE
French, 1860–1945
Pendant-brooch with pink carnations, 1901–2
Gold, enamel, pink sapphire, and cast glass

45

3
Rᴇɴᴇ́ Lᴀʟɪᴏ̨ᴜᴇ
French, 1860-1945
Floral brooch, 1901-2
Gold, enamel, diamond,
and cast glass

Fig. 22 (opposite, detail)
Arthur Illies (German,
1870-1952), *Jelänger-Jelieber
(Honeysuckle)*, 1896, color
etching on cream Asian
paper

5
RENÉ LALIQUE
French, 1860–1945
Hair comb with ivy leaves,
1902–3
Gold, enamel, sapphire,
and horn

6 (front and back)
RENÉ LALIQUE
French, 1860-1945
Carnation watch, 1898-1900
Gold, enamel, and crystal

7
RENÉ LALIQUE
French, 1860–1945
Dog collar plaque with a
floral motif, 1899–1901
Gold, enamel, and diamond

8
René Lalique
French, 1860–1945
*Branch brooch with cherry
blossoms*, 1900–1902
Gold, diamond, and cast glass

Fig. 23 (opposite)
Daum frères (French, established 1875), *Vase*, 1910–15,
glass

9
French, 1860–1945
Vine and berries hair comb,
about 1900
Gold and ivory

10 (opposite)
RENÉ LALIQUE
French, 1860–1945
*Fringe necklace with blister
pearls*, about 1902–3
Gold, enamel, and pearl

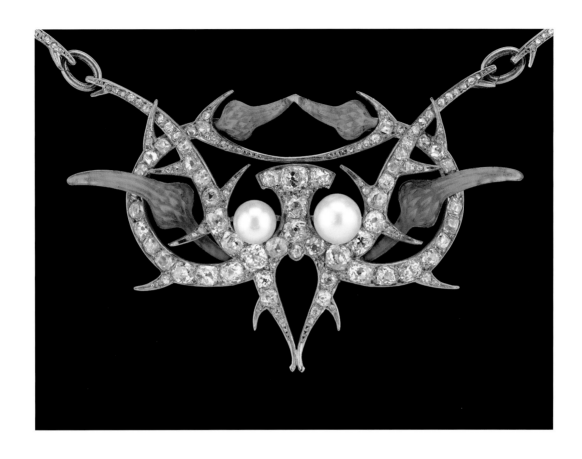

11
René Lalique
French, 1860–1945
Thistle necklace, 1904–5
Gold, enamel, diamond,
pearl, and cast glass

12
RENÉ LALIQUE
French, 1860-1945
Belt buckle, about 1900
Gold, enamel, and opal

13
RENÉ LALIQUE
French, 1860–1945
Flowering tree brooch,
about 1910
Steel

14
René Lalique
French, 1860–1945
Dog collar plaques with carnations, 1899–1900
Gold, enamel, diamond, pearl, and topaz

Fig. 24 (opposite, detail)
Eugène Grasset (French, born in Switzerland, 1841–1917), *Iris*, plate from *Plants and Their Application to Ornament*, 1897, illustrated book with 72 color lithographs

15 (top and bottom)
RENÉ LALIQUE
French, 1860-1945
Box with olive tree motif,
about 1900
Gold, enamel, and smoky
quartz

René Lalique
French, 1860–1945
*Pendant-brooch with a
village scene*, about 1900
Platinum, gold, enamel,
and diamond

17
RENÉ LALIQUE
French, 1860–1945
Lily-of-the-valley necklace,
about 1920
Gold and cast glass

18
LOUIS ZORRA
Possibly born in Italy, working
in Paris
*Brooch with an opal and
pearl*, about 1900
Gold, silver, enamel, sapphire,
opal, and pearl

19 (opposite)
LUCIEN GAILLARD
French, 1861–1933
Necklace with bleeding hearts,
about 1907
Gold and enamel

20
Designed by
CHARLES DESROSIERS, French
For GEORGES FOUQUET
French, 1862–1957
Orchid brooch, 1898–1901
Gold, enamel, diamond, and pearl

Fig. 25 (opposite, detail)
E. A. Séguy, *Orchidées*,
pochoir print, plate number
28 from *Les fleurs et leurs
applications décoratives*
(Paris: A. Calavas, 1902)

21
Designed by
CHARLES DESROSIERS, French
For GEORGES FOUQUET
French, 1862–1957
*Brooch with leaves and
blossoms*, 1901
Gold, enamel, diamond, and
baroque pearl

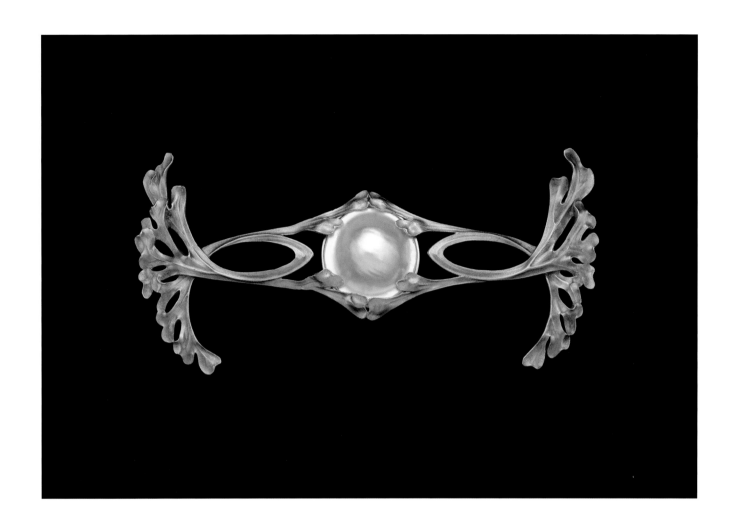

22
PAUL LIÉNARD
French, 1849–?
Seaweed brooch, about 1908
Gold and mabe pearl

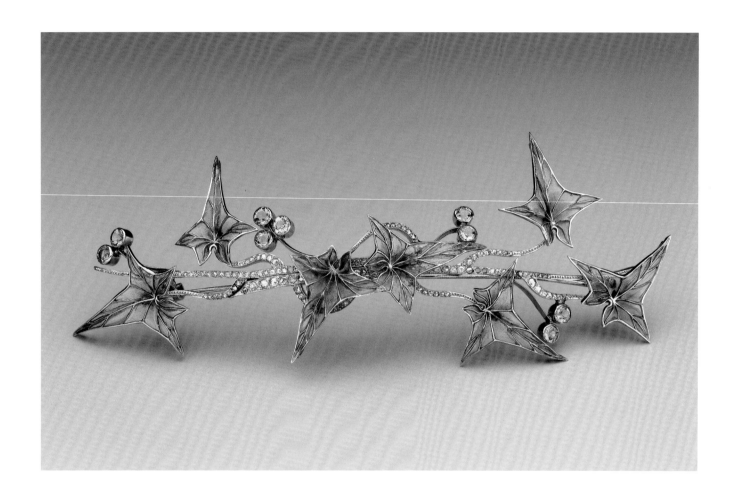

23
<small>UNKNOWN MAKER</small>
Possibly Austrian
Ivy brooch, about 1900
Platinum, gold, enamel,
diamond, and peridot

24
UNKNOWN MAKER
American
Orchid pendant, about 1905
Gold, enamel, diamond, and
pearl

26
KARL ROTHMÜLLER
German, 1860–1930
Pendant necklace, about 1910
Gold, silver, enamel, green
stone, red stone, and pearl

28
LÉOPOLD ALBERT MARIN
GAUTRAIT
French, 1865–1937
For LÉON GARIOD, French
*Pendant necklace with
carnations*, 1904
Gold, enamel, and diamond

29
UNKNOWN MAKER
French
Brooch with bamboo stalks and leaves, about 1900
Gold, enamel, opal, and glass

30 (below)
FUSET GRAU
Probably Spanish
Bracelet with scrolls and leaves, about 1900
Platinum, gold, diamond, and citrine

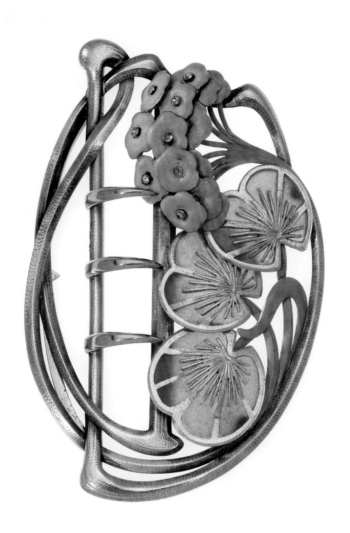

31
HENRI VEVER
French, 1854-1942
*Belt buckle with lily pads
and blossoms*, about 1900
Gold, enamel, and diamond

FRANK GARDNER HALE
American, 1876–1945
Pendant, about 1910
Gold, diamond, and green
tourmaline

33
Possibly by
EMMANUEL-JULES-JOSEPH
(JOË) DESCOMPS
French, 1872–1948
Pendant with blossoms,
about 1900
Gold, enamel, and emerald

Fauna

34
RENÉ LALIQUE
French, 1860–1945
For HENRI VEVER, French,
1854–1942, and PAUL VEVER,
French, 1850–1915
Swallow brooch, 1889
Gold, silver, enamel, diamond,
and ruby

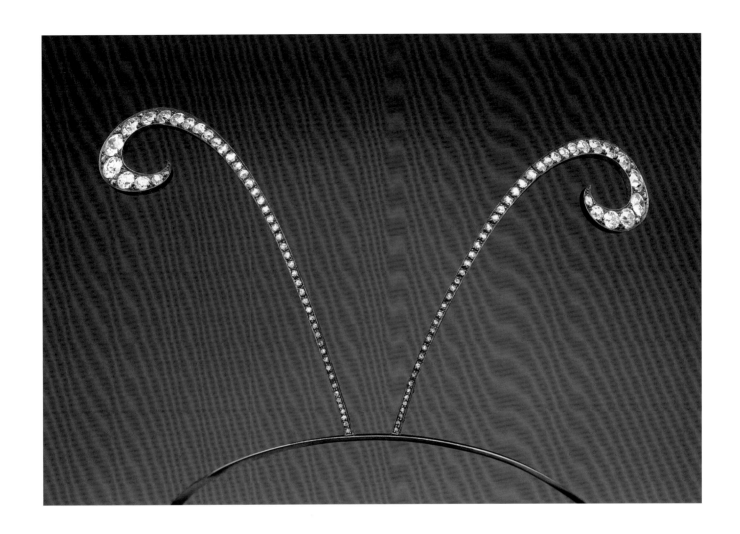

35
RENÉ LALIQUE
French, 1860–1945
*Hair ornament with
antennae*, about 1900
Gold, silver, steel, and
diamond

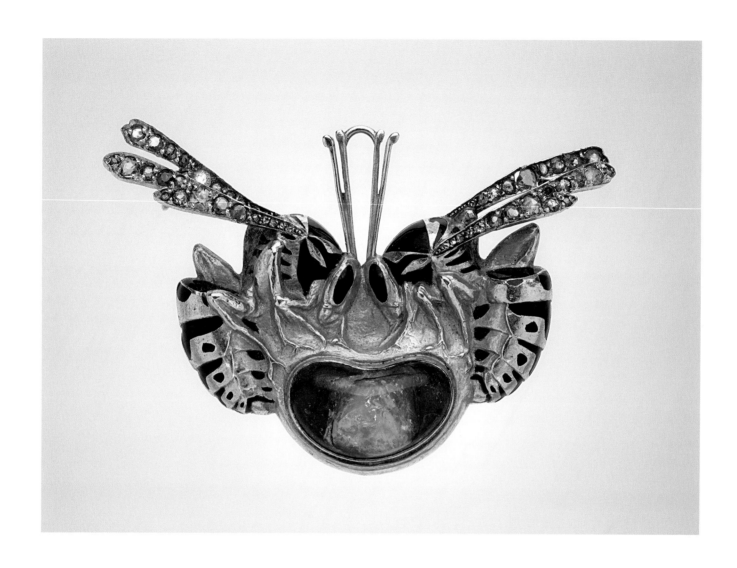

36
René Lalique
French, 1860–1945
Pendant-brooch with wasps,
about 1900
Gold, enamel, diamond,
emerald, ruby, sapphire,
and opal

90

37
RENÉ LALIQUE
French, 1860–1945
Brooch with rooster,
1898–1900
Gold and enamel

38
PHILIPPE WOLFERS
Belgian, 1858–1929
"Dragonfly" pendant-brooch, 1904
Platinum, gold, enamel, diamond,
ruby, and pearl

Fig. 26
Yoshimori (Japanese),
Dragonflies and Grasses,
1857, woodblock print

39
<small>UNKNOWN MAKER</small>
French
Moth brooch, about 1900
Gold, enamel, diamond,
and pearl

94

40
Unknown maker
Probably American
*En tremblant dragonfly
brooch*, about 1900
Platinum, gold, enamel,
diamond, emerald, and ruby

41
Probably by LOUIS AUCOC
French, 1850-1932
Butterfly brooch, about 1900
Platinum, gold, enamel,
emerald, ruby, sapphire,
and horn

42
Louis Aucoc
French, 1850–1932
Dragonfly brooch, about 1900
Platinum, gold, enamel,
diamond, emerald, ruby,
and horn

Fig. 27
Unknown artist (French),
Folding fan, about 1905, silk
satin leaf painted in watercolor, embroidered with
sequins, with ivory sticks
and steel rivet and ring

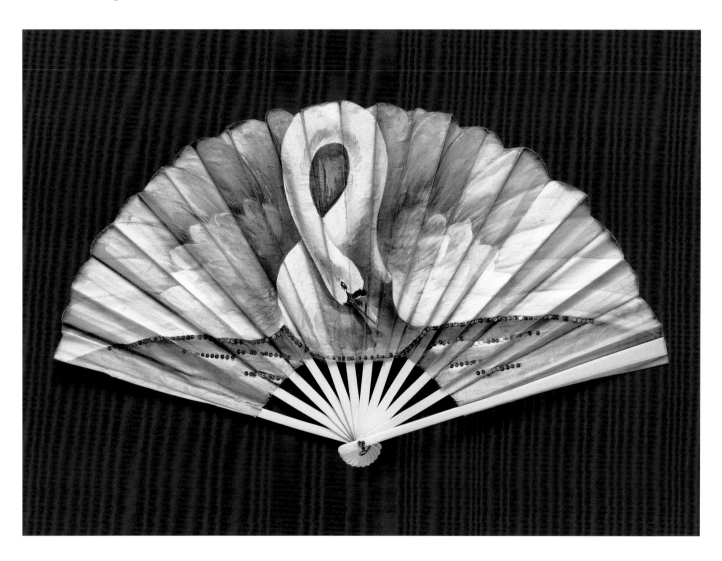

43
LÉOPOLD ALBERT MARIN
GAUTRAIT
French, 1865–1937
For LÉON GARIOD, French
*Pendant necklace with two
swans*, about 1900
Gold, enamel, diamond, pearl,
and peridot

44
Victor Gérard
French
Retailed by Louchet
French
Pendant necklace with swallows, about 1900
Gold and enamel

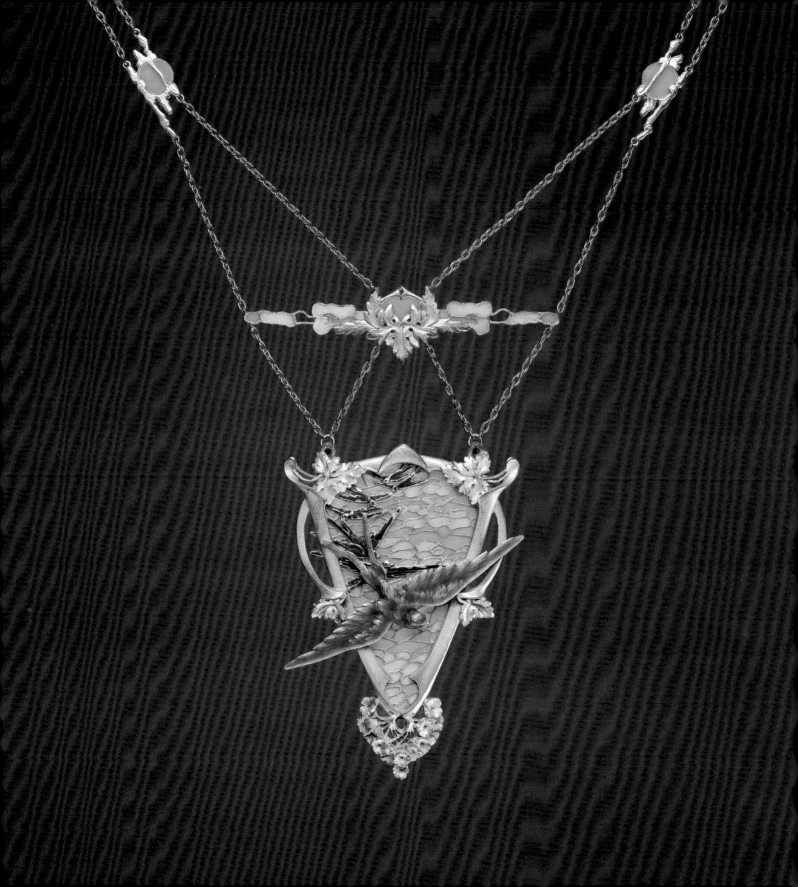

Fig. 28 (detail)
William H. Bradley
(American, 1868–1962),
*"The Modern Poster" for
Scribner's*, 1895, relief
process printed in color

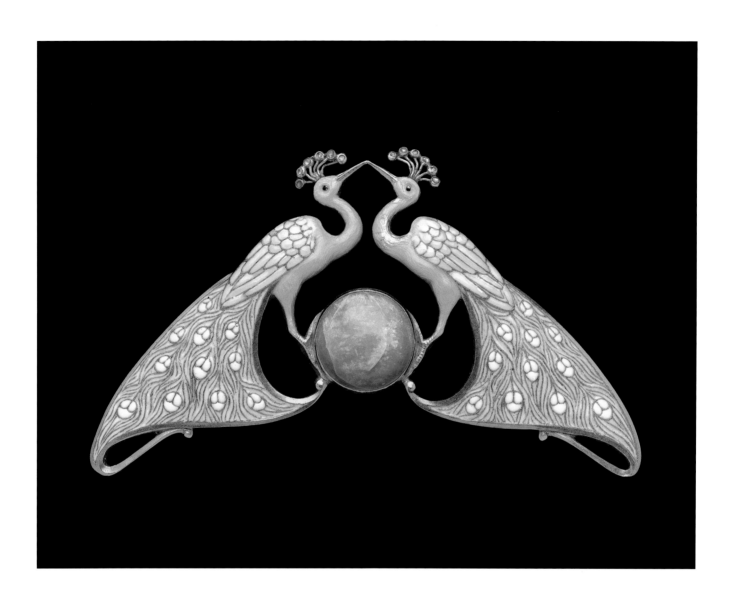

46
EUGÈNE FEUILLÂTRE
French, 1870–1916
Double peacock necklace,
about 1900
Gold, enamel, diamond,
and opal

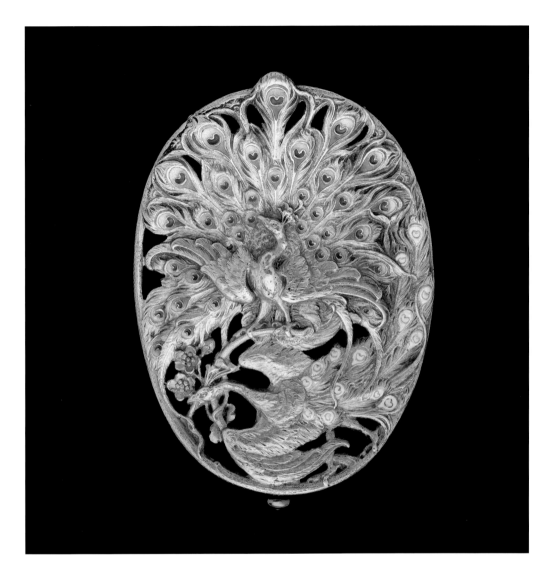

47
GEORGES FOUQUET
French, 1862–1957
Belt buckle with two peacocks,
about 1900
Gold and enamel

LUCIEN GAILLARD
French, 1861–1933
Beetle necklace, about 1900
Gold, patinated silver,
enamel, diamond, and pearl

49
MAURICE-PHILIPPE FOURAIN
French
Pendant necklace with two intertwined serpents, 1911
Gold, silver, aquamarine, and ivory

Fig. 29 (detail)
Otto Eckmann (German,
1865-1902), *Fünf Schwane*
(Five Swans), 1897, tapestry-
woven wool and cotton

50
GUSTAVE-ROGER SANDOZ
French, 1867–?
Pendant-brooch with a pond scene and two swans,
about 1900
Gold and enamel

51
LUCIEN HIRTZ
French, 1864–1928
Probably made by GUSTAVE
ESPINASSE, French
Gem carved by BURDY, French
For FRÉDÉRIC BOUCHERON
French, 1830–1902
Belt buckle with lionesses,
1900
Gold, emerald, and garnet

52 (opposite)
UNKNOWN MAKER
French
*Egyptian-revival tiara comb
and bracelet*, about 1900
Gold, enamel, ruby, sapphire,
and glazed steatite (ancient
Egyptian scarabs)

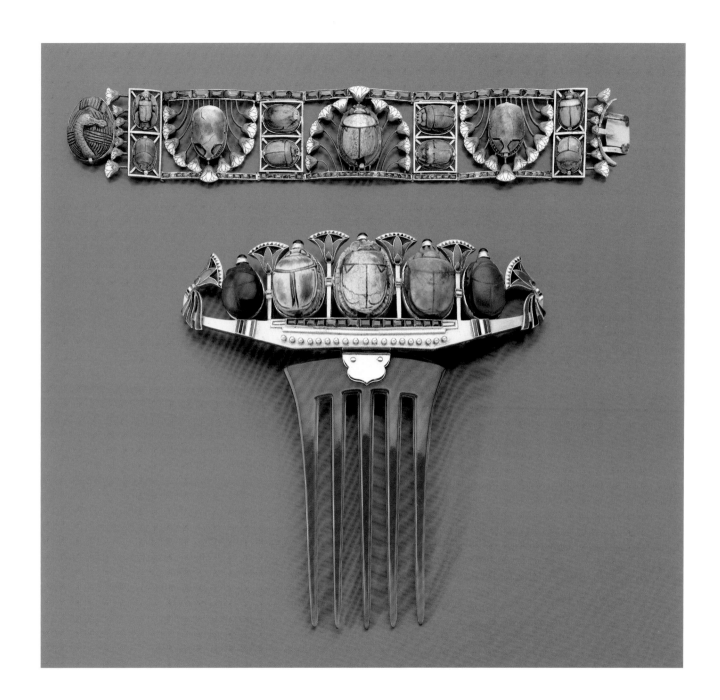

53
F. WALTER LAWRENCE
American, 1864-1929
*Dog collar with a nautical
scene*, about 1903
Gold and pearl

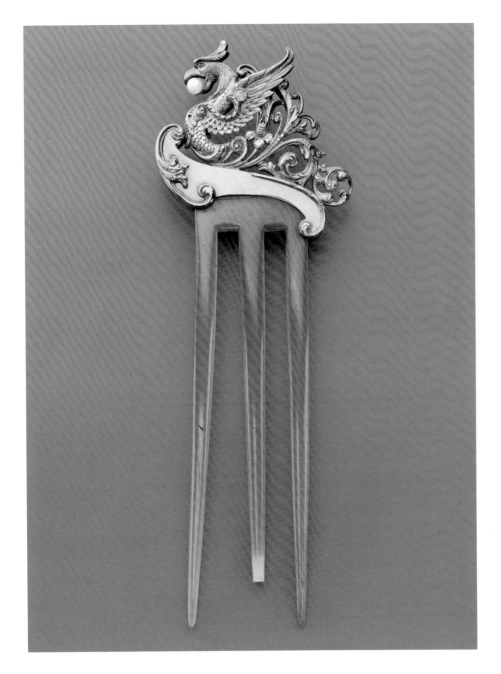

54
<small>UNKNOWN MAKER</small>
American
*Hair comb with a profile
dragon on a wave*, about 1910
Gold, emerald, ruby, pearl,
and horn

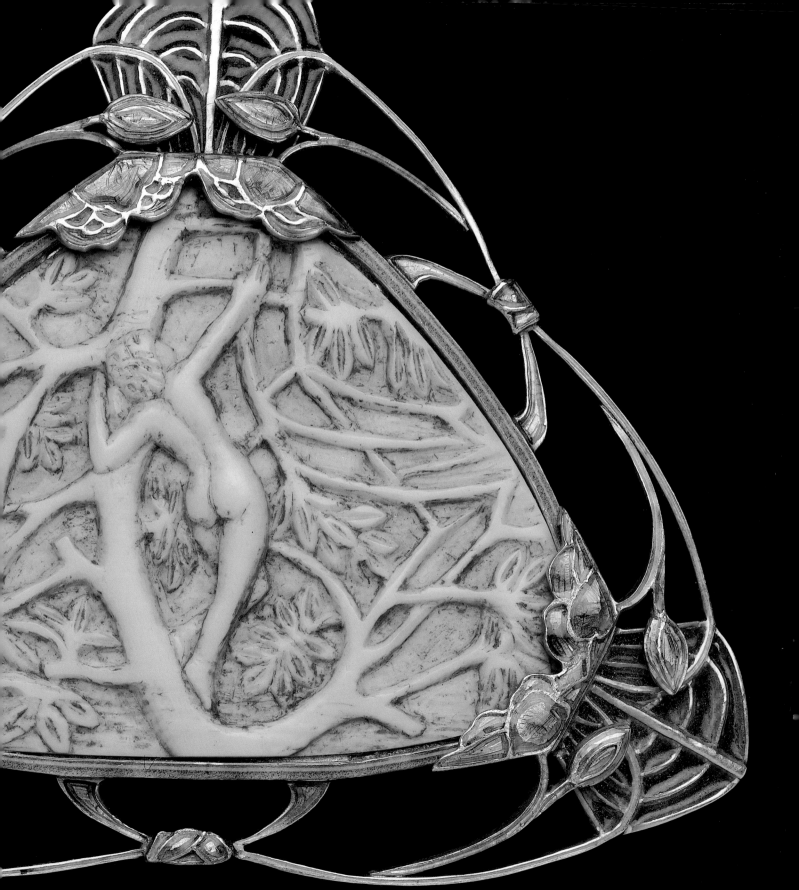

THE HUMAN FIGURE

55
RENÉ LALIQUE
French, 1860–1945
Pendant necklace with a
figure of Flora, 1904–5
Gold, opal, and *pâte de verre*
glass

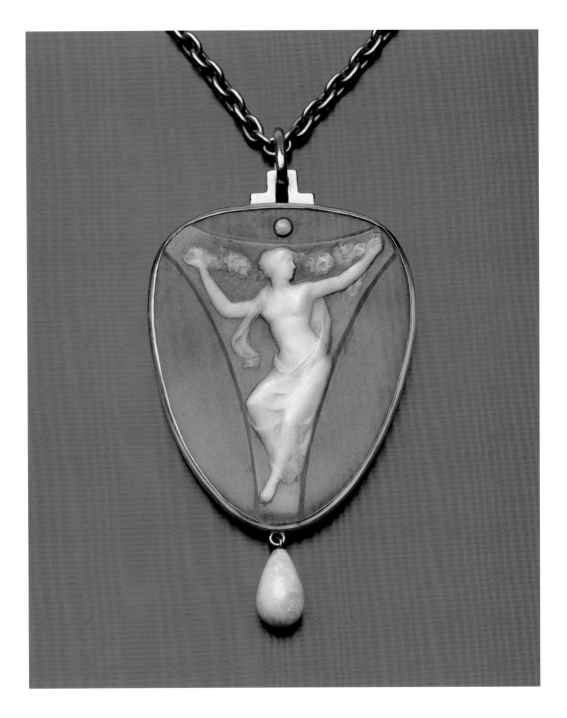

56
RENÉ LALIQUE
French, 1860-1945
*Pendant necklace with three
female figures*, 1904-5
Gold, peridot, and engraved
glass

BAKST
1913

57
RENÉ LALIQUE
French, 1860-1945
Brooch with a female figure,
about 1903
Gold, enamel, and diamond

Fig. 30 (opposite)
Léon Nikolaievitch Bakst
(Russian, 1866-1924),
Madame Bartet as Bérénice,
1913, watercolor, gouache,
gold paint, and graphite
pencil on paper

58
RENÉ LALIQUE
French, 1860–1945
*Brooch with dancing nymphs
in butterfly frame*, 1901–2
Gold, enamel, sapphire, and
cast glass

59
RENÉ LALIQUE
French, 1860-1945
Hair comb with female figures and thistles, about 1901-2
Silver, horn, and *pâte de verre* glass

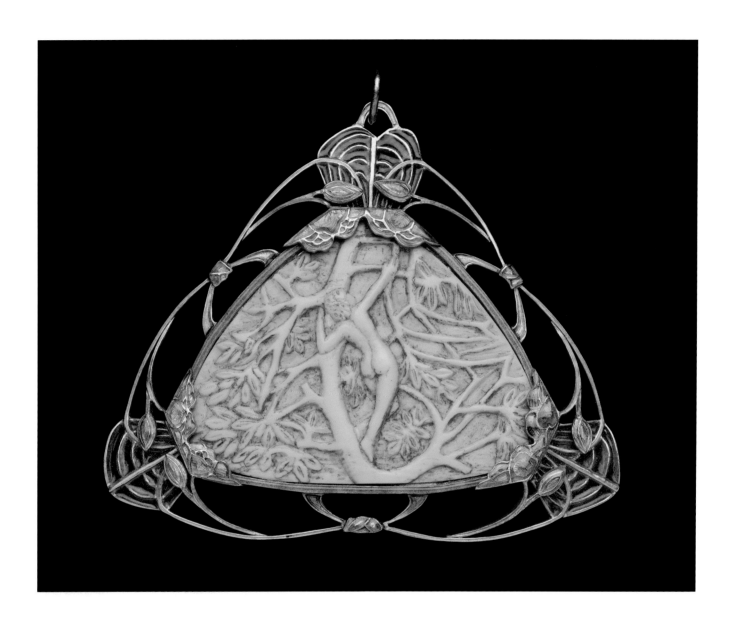

60
RENÉ LALIQUE
French, 1860–1945
Pendant with wood nymph,
1904–5
Gold, enamel, and artificial
ivory

61
René Lalique
French, 1860–1945
*Handle with sweet pea and
a female bust*, 1899–1900
Gold, enamel, and cast glass

Probably by LOUIS AUCOC
French, 1850–1932
*Pendant-brooch with a
female bust*, about 1900
Gold, enamel, and pearl

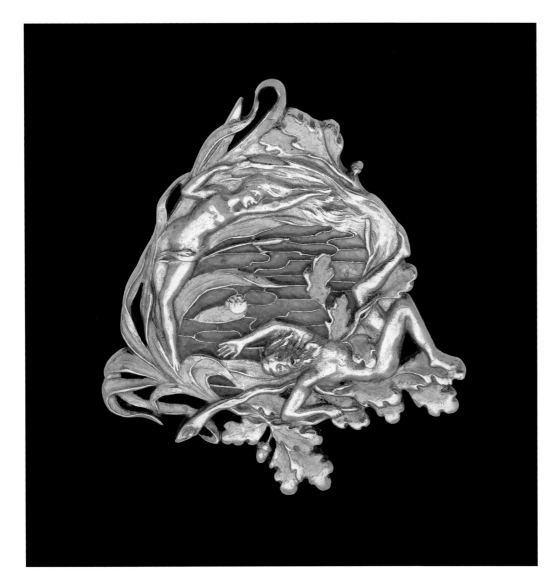

63
ANDRÉ RAMBOUR
French
*Pendant with a water scene
and two figures*, about 1900
Gold and enamel

64
UNKNOWN MAKER
Probably French
*Pendant with a female head
in a sheep frame*, about 1900
Gold, diamond, and pearl

Mold for the pendant, about
1900
Wood

65
EDMOND-HENRI BECKER,
relief plaque
French, 1871–?
LOUIS AUCOC, frame
French, 1850–1932
*Brooch with children in a
floral frame*, 1899
Gold and enamel

66
Probably French
*Pendant-brooch with a marsh
fairy*, about 1900
Gold, enamel, and amethyst

67
PHILIPPE WOLFERS
Belgian, 1858–1929
"Night" pendant-brooch,
about 1899
Gold, enamel, opal, pearl,
and cast glass

68
EMMANUEL-JULES-JOSEPH
(JOË) DESCOMPS
French, 1872–1948
For LÉON GARIOD, French
*Pendant necklace with a
female head and a sphinx*,
about 1900
Gold, enamel, diamond, and
pearl

Fig. 31 (opposite)
Jan Toorop (Dutch, 1858–
1928), *Panis Angelicus*, 1894,
pastel, applied wet, over
graphite on tan wove paper

COMTE ENGUERRAND DU
SUAU DE LA CROIX, frame
French
LOUIS OSCAR ROTY, medal
French, 1846–1911
Wedding medallion, 1901
(medal designed in 1895)
Gilt silver, silver, enamel,
diamond, and pearl

70
LÉOPOLD ALBERT MARIN
GAUTRAIT
French, 1865–1937
For LÉON GARIOD, French
*Pendant-brooch with a
female head*, about 1900
Gold, enamel, diamond,
opal, and pearl

71
UNKNOWN MAKER
Possibly American
*Pendant with a female profile
head*, about 1900
Gold, silver, and enamel

73
UNKNOWN MAKER
French
Pendant-brooch with a female head, about 1900
Platinum, gold, enamel, diamond, and ruby

74 (opposite)
ALIX ANGENOT
French
Purse, about 1900
Gold, silk, and metallic thread

75
CHARLES-RENÉ IHM
French
*Hair comb–brooch with
woman and peacock*, 1901
Gold, enamel, opal, and
tortoiseshell

Fig. 32 (detail)
William H. Bradley
(American, 1868–1962),
*Poster for Bradley—His Book
(Woman and Blue Peacock)*,
1896, relief process printed
in color

76
EMMANUEL-JULES-JOSEPH
(JOË) DESCOMPS
French, 1872–1948
Pendant necklace with wood nymph, about 1900
Gold, enamel, diamond, pearl, and peridot

140

77
UNKNOWN MAKER
Birth of Venus pendant,
about 1900
Gold, enamel, and pearl

78
RIKER BROTHERS
American, working
1892–1926
Brooch with a female head
with curvilinear tresses,
about 1900
Gold, enamel, and diamond

79
VLADIMIR SOLOVIEV
Russian
For PETER CARL FABERGÉ
Russian, 1846-1920
Pendant locket with a female
head in a ribbon frame,
1905-10
Gold, diamond, and ruby

ARTIST BIOGRAPHIES

Susan Ward

Note to the reader

All quotations in this section are taken from Henri Vever, *La bijouterie française au XIXe siècle*, 3 vols. (1906–8), published in English as *French Jewelry of the Nineteenth Century* (London: Thames & Hudson, 2001).

When available, birth and death dates are listed under the artist's name; some artists' dates are not known.

Angenot, Alix

French jeweler, apparently one of a family of jewelers, with an atelier at 18, rue Chapon, Paris. His maker's mark was registered between 1882 and 1901. The firm also had marks registered under the names "Angenot & Cie" from 1876 to 1885 and "Angenot frères" from 1901 to 1911. It was mentioned by Henri Vever as one of "many distinguished old or new firms" working in Paris during the Third Republic.

Aucoc, Louis (fils)

1850–1932

French jeweler and son of a well-known Paris goldsmith, Louis Aucoc *ainé* (the elder); his brother, André, was also a goldsmith. In 1877 he took over the Maison Lobjois at 9, rue du Quatre Septembre and founded the Maison Louis Aucoc. He participated in national and international exhibitions beginning in 1878 and was a member of the jury for the 1889 and 1900 Expositions universelles in Paris. From 1895 to 1907, Aucoc served as president of the professional association of Parisian goldsmiths and jewelers, the Chambre syndicale de la bijouterie-joaillerie-orfèvrerie, and was active in organizing and promoting exhibitions and competitions. He was Lalique's teacher and first employer, from 1876 to 1878. After his retirement in 1907, the firm continued until the mid-1920s under the direction of his son Georges.

Becker, Edmond-Henri

1871–?

French sculptor, medalist, woodcarver, and jeweler who exhibited at the Salon of the Societé des artistes français from 1898 to 1914, winning a second-class medal in 1902 and a first-class medal in 1911. His medals, designs, and models, often featuring delicate low-relief portraits of women and children, were used by many Paris jewelers, most notably Louis Aucoc, Boucheron, and Ferdinand Verger.

Boucheron

Paris jewelry firm founded by Frédéric Boucheron (1830–1902). Boucheron apprenticed with Jules Chaise and worked for the firm Tixier-Deschamps before opening his own workshop in the Palais-Royal in 1858. He exhibited at national and international exhibitions beginning in 1866, and his work attracted attention for its originality of design, excellent workmanship, and use of unusual materials. He was one of the first jewelers to work with *plique à jour* enamel, in the 1860s. Boucheron employed a series of talented designers, including Jules Debut (from 1858 to 1879), Paul Legrand (1863 to 1892), and Lucien Hirtz (1893 to 1928), and also commissioned work from other firms and from freelance artists and designers. He received a grand prix for his display at the 1900 Exposition universelle, which included cat. 51. In 1893 the Maison Boucheron moved to the place Vendôme; after Frédéric's death, in 1902, his son, Louis, took over the firm. The Boucheron family directed the company until 2000, and Louis's grandson Alain remains associated with it.

Brandt, Paul-Emile

1883–1952

French jeweler and metalworker born in Chaux-de-Fonds, Switzerland. Brandt moved to Paris to study and established a shop in the rue des Saints-Pères. He exhibited in the 1908 Exposition de la parure précieuse de la femme at the Musée Galliera and at the Salon des artistes français, where he won an honorable mention in 1906, a third-class medal in 1911, and a gold medal in 1923. His Art Nouveau jewelry designs often featured flowers and/or insects, and many incorporated carved opal elements. In the 1920s and 1930s, he created boldly geometric jewelry and cigarette cases in the Art Deco style, often contrasting diamonds with onyx or black enamel, or multicolored lacquer with silver.

Descomps, Emmanuel-Jules-Joseph (Joë)

1872–1948

French sculptor, medalist, and engraver. Descomps studied sculpture with Louis-Auguste Hiolin and trained in Paris with the firm of jeweler Gabriel Falguières. He exhibited regularly at the Salon of the Societé des artistes français, of which he became a member in 1893, receiving an honorable mention in 1898, a third-class medal in 1921, a second-class medal in 1925, and a first-class medal in 1928. He also exhibited at the 1902 Salon of the Société nationale des beaux-arts and at the 1908 Exposition de la parure précieuse de la femme. Descomps designed jewelry, usually combining sculpted and engraved goldwork with enamels, for his own workshop and for other jewelers, most notably Léon Gariod, Paul Louchet, and André Rambour. His workshop was first located at 399, rue des Pyrénées, moving to 37, rue du Moulin Vert in 1900. He was also known as a designer of statuettes, vases, and other decorative objects, and in the 1920s he created bronze and ivory figure statues in the Art Deco style.

Desrosiers, Charles

French designer, student of designer and graphic artist Eugène Grasset (who designed jewelry for Vever) and of painter and graphic artist Luc-Olivier Merson. Between 1898 and 1914, he worked for Georges Fouquet, designing nearly all of the jewelry produced by Fouquet during that time. His sophisticated, organic designs, often featuring opals and baroque pearls, were in large part responsible for Fouquet's leading status among Art Nouveau jewelers.

Espinasse, Gustave

French goldsmith and jeweler who made pieces for the Maison Boucheron (including cat. 51) from approximately 1900 to 1908. His workshop was located at 79, rue des Petits-Champs. His mark was registered from 1896 until he was succeeded by Edouard Thullier in 1911.

Fabergé, Peter Carl

1846–1920

Jeweler and goldsmith to the Russian imperial court, best known for creating jeweled "objects of fantasy," such as the annual imperial Easter eggs. The house of Fabergé was founded in 1842 in Saint Petersburg by Gustave Fabergé (1814–1894) and at first produced fashionable, traditional jewelry. Gustave's son Peter Carl took over the business in 1870 and changed the direction of the firm, introducing finely crafted and embellished objets d'art such as clocks, cigarette cases, and picture frames. In 1885 Fabergé received the title Supplier to the Imperial Court and produced the first imperial Easter egg, ordered by Czar Alexander III. Fabergé's reputation spread abroad through exhibitions in Germany and Sweden and through his dis-

play at the 1900 Exposition universelle, which included several of the imperial Easter presents. The firm employed many talented jewelers and craftsmen (up to seven hundred between 1907 and 1917), organized into specialized workshops under the direction of work masters, who earned the right to mark pieces with their own initials in addition to the Fabergé mark. Fabergé opened shops and workshops in Moscow in 1887, Odessa in 1890, and Kiev in 1905, inaugurating its only foreign branch in London in 1903. Although most of Fabergé's objects and jewels were eighteenth-century or Neoclassical in style, some pieces show the influence of Art Nouveau, particularly around 1910. In 1918, after the Russian Revolution, Fabergé's workshops in Saint Petersburg were closed; he escaped the country and died two years later in Switzerland.

Feuillâtre, Eugène

1870–1916

French goldsmith, sculptor, and enameler. Feuillâtre is thought to have begun an apprenticeship with a goldsmith at an early age and to have studied with the enamelers Etienne Tourette and Louis Houillon. He was the head of René Lalique's enamel workshop from 1890 to 1897 and established his own workshop at 3, rue de Villedo, Paris, in 1898. From 1898 to 1914, he regularly exhibited jewelry and decorative objects at the Salon des artistes français and the Salon of the Société des artistes décorateurs. He also participated in international shows, including the Exposition universelle in 1900 (where he received a gold medal), and exhibited with the Belgian society Libre esthétique in Brussels and with Lalique and Fouquet at the New Gallery in London. Feuillâtre became famous for his skill and technical experimentation as an enameler and for the highly original vases and boxes, in translucent enamel over silver, that he created around 1900–1910.

Fouquet, Georges

1862–1957

French jeweler, one of the leading creators of jewelry in both the Art Nouveau and Art Deco styles. He was the eldest son of the Paris goldsmith and jeweler Alphonse Fouquet, who was well known for his designs inspired by antique and Renaissance models. Georges Fouquet worked for his father beginning in 1880 and took over the firm, then located at 35, avenue de l'Opéra, in 1895. Open to new ideas, he changed the company's direction, exhibiting his first pieces in the Art Nouveau style at the Salon des artistes français in 1898 (including an orchid brooch in the same design as cat. 20). In 1898 he also began a fruitful collaboration with Charles Desrosiers, who designed nearly all of the pieces made by the firm between 1898 and 1914. At about the same time, he began to employ the master enameler Etienne Tourette, who was known for creating shimmering effects (sometimes by etching the surface of the enamel with acid) and for including tiny pieces of gold leaf (paillons) in his enamels. Between 1899 and 1901, Fouquet also commissioned designs from the painter and graphic artist Alphonse Mucha. Mucha designed spectacular pieces for actress Sarah Bernhardt and for Fouquet's display at the 1900 Exposition universelle, which received a gold medal. Between 1900 and 1901, Mucha also designed the dramatic facade and interiors for Fouquet's new showroom at 6, rue Royale. Around 1910 Fouquet's jewelry grew lighter and more classical in inspiration, and he became known as "the father of the aquamarine" because of his fondness for that stone. In the 1920s Fouquet successfully adapted to the Art Deco style; some of the boldest pieces were the work of his son, Jean, who designed for him between 1925 and 1931. Fouquet served as president of the jewelry section of the 1925 Exposition internationale des arts décoratifs et industriels modernes, and in 1934 he organized the publication of an important monograph on modern jewelry design. The difficult financial climate of the 1930s led him to close his doors in 1936.

Fourain, Maurice-Philippe

French jeweler who exhibited his jewelry at the Salon des artistes français in 1909, 1910, and 1911 (including cat. 49) and the Salon des artistes décorateurs in 1910.

Fuset Grau

Very little is known about this mark, which is thought to be that of a Spanish maker (possibly from Barcelona or Valencia).

Gaillard, Lucien

1861-1933

Innovative French jeweler and goldsmith, known particularly for his interest in Japanese design and techniques. He was the son of goldsmith Ernest Gaillard, whose firm (founded by his father, Amédée Gaillard, in 1840) was located at 101, rue du Temple, Paris. During the 1870s, Ernest Gaillard began to make small decorative items and accessories in the Japanese taste and to experiment with mixed-metal ornamentation. He won a silver medal for this work at the Exposition universelle of 1878. At the same exhibition, Lucien Gaillard, who had just joined his father's firm as an apprentice, became fascinated by the Japanese metalwork on display and was determined to discover the secrets of Japanese manufacturing processes. In 1881 he began a serious study of Japanese techniques, and for the rest of his career he constantly experimented with alloys, patination, lacquer, and complex mixed-metal inlay techniques. He won a gold medal for his metalwork at the 1889 Exposition universelle and took over his father's firm in 1892. In the late 1890s, inspired by the work of René Lalique, he began to design jewelry and hair combs, for which he received a gold medal at the 1900 Exposition universelle. In that year he relocated to a large workshop and showroom at 107, rue de la Boetie and recruited a number of craftsmen from Japan. Gaillard exhibited at the Salon des artistes français between 1901 and 1909, receiving a first-class medal in 1904. He made many combs and hairpins of carved horn, which were praised for their sensitive designs and distinctive tints and patinas.

Gariod, Léon

French jeweler. In 1875 he merged with the firm founded in 1859 by Gaucher and Tonnelier at 29, rue Saint-Augustin, Paris, and in 1884 he registered the business under his own name. At first he was known as a specialist in gold chains and flexible bracelets set with precious stones. From 1897 to about 1905, he collaborated with designer and modeler Léopold Albert Marin Gautrait on pendants and brooches in the Art Nouveau style. Henri Vever described these as "charming works of rare perfection in which chasing and enameling play a large part," and he praised their "great refinement." Gariod also executed designs by Joë Descomps during this period. Gariod and Gautrait continued to collaborate until 1920, but after 1905 Gautrait abandoned Art Nouveau for Louis XVI-revival designs. Some of their works may have been retailed by other jewelers, such as Vever.

Gautrait, Léopold Albert Marin

1865-1937

French sculptor and designer. He studied with M. Rouffosse at the Ecole des beaux-arts, Paris, and exhibited a wax model for a gilt-bronze vase at the 1894 Salon des artistes français. From 1897 to about 1905, he designed and chased jewelry in the Art Nouveau style for the jeweler Léon Gariod. The majority of these pieces were pendants and brooches in finely chased gold and enamel, with precious stones used as accents. Gautrait's jewels are distinguished by their crisp, lively quality and by his ability to seamlessly integrate into his designs multiple loops for attaching chains and pendant drops. Many necklaces also feature a starburst element above the main pendant. Although some extant pieces are marked only with Gautrait's signature (without Gariod's maker's mark), most of these are thought to have been made by Gariod. Around 1905 Gautrait began to work in a Louis XVI-revival style, and he appears to have sold most of the models for his Art Nouveau designs to a German jeweler in Pforzheim (some of these were reissued in the 1970s).

Gautrait worked with Gariod until 1920 and continued to make pieces for private clients until 1930.

Gérard, Victor

French jeweler/fabricator. His maker's mark was registered between 1899 and 1930, and his workshop was located first at 42, boulevard de Sébastopol and later at 29, rue de Richelieu. Although the jewels bearing his mark are of very high quality, little is known about him. It may be that he fabricated pieces primarily for other jewelers and retailers, such as Paul Louchet (see cat. 44), rather than retailing jewelry under his own name.

Hale, Frank Gardner

1876-1945

American jeweler, enameler, and designer considered a key figure in the American Arts and Crafts movement. Hale was born in Norwich, Connecticut, and studied at the Norwich Art School and the School of the Museum of Fine Arts, Boston. Initially he designed book covers, book plates, and covers for sheet music, before going to England in 1906 to study metalwork and jewelry making at C. R. Ashbee's Guild of Handicraft at Chipping Camden and jewelry and enameling with Fred Partridge in London. In 1907 he returned to Boston, opened a studio at 2 Park Square, and became a member of the Society of Arts and Crafts, Boston; he was active with the SACB for many years as a council and jury member, and as vice president in 1926. His work was exhibited around the country and received numerous awards, including a silver medal at the 1915 Panama-Pacific International Exposition in San Francisco, the SACB's Medal of Excellence in 1915, and the Logan Prize at the Exhibition of Applied Arts at the Art Institute of Chicago in 1917. Hale also lectured extensively, founded the Jewelers' Guild in 1919, and trained numerous apprentices, including Edward Everett Oakes. He was praised for his meticulous craftsmanship and for his harmonious, original, and carefully structured designs.

Hirtz, Lucien

1864–1928

French designer and enameler. He began his career designing jewelry for Alexis Falize, before moving to Boucheron in 1893. From 1893 to 1928, he designed jewelry, silver and gold objects, and enameled objects and plaques for Boucheron, becoming known as both a skilled modeler and one of the finest enamelers and colorists of the day. Hirtz exhibited regularly at the Salon des Beaux-Arts between 1896 and 1914, and his work for Boucheron at the 1900 Exposition universelle (including cat. 51) was much admired. For the 1925 Exposition internationale des arts décoratifs et industriels modernes, he created jewelry in the Art Deco style, featuring unexpected combinations of materials such as coral and lapis lazuli.

Ihm, Charles-René

French jeweler who exhibited his work at the Salon des artistes français in 1901 (including cat. 75).

Lalique, René

1860–1945

Innovative French jewelry and glass designer; the most important creator of Art Nouveau jewelry. Born in Ay, Lalique apprenticed with jeweler and goldsmith Louis Aucoc (*fils*) from 1876 to 1878 and attended the Ecole des arts décoratifs for some months, before studying for two years at Sydenham College in London. In 1880 he returned to Paris and began supplying designs to Paris jewelers, including Aucoc, Destape, Cartier, and Gariod; he also designed fans, carpets, and textiles. In 1882–83, he took a modeling course given by sculptor Justin Lequien at the Ecole Bernard Palissy and also studied etching. In 1885 he took over the atelier of Jules Destape, on the place Baillon, and over the next several years he created gem-set jewelry for other houses, including Cartier, Boucheron, and Vever. By 1890, when he moved his workshop to 20, rue Thérèse, he was already employing about thir-

ty craftsmen. At about this time, Lalique began experimenting with novel materials such as horn, ivory, enamel, and glass, which he valued for their artistic possibilities, harmoniously combining them with precious stones such as rubies, opals, and diamonds. He also began to explore a new aesthetic, which was strongly influenced by Japanese art, based on naturalistically rendered flowers, trees, animals, and insects and on Symbolist themes such as serpents, sphinxes, or insect-women. In 1894 he designed some dramatic stage jewelry for the actress Sarah Bernhardt, and the following year he began to exhibit his jewelry at the Salon des artistes français; he showed jewelry there regularly until 1910. Lalique exhibited at numerous international exhibitions, including those in Brussels (1897), where we won a grand prix, Munich (1899), Turin (1902 and 1910), London (1903 and 1905), Berlin (1903), and Saint Louis (1904). His work was widely published, and he was credited with being the inventor of a new kind of jewelry, which became known as "genre Lalique." His greatest success came at the 1900 Exposition universelle, where his spectacular display of jewelry received a grand prix and sealed his reputation. In 1902 Lalique moved his home and workshops to 40, cours la Reine, and in 1905 he opened a shop in the place Vendôme. Around 1901 glass began to play a more important role in his jewelry and decorative work, and later in the decade he began to concentrate on glass almost exclusively. In 1909 he created his first perfume bottles for François Coty, took over a glassworks in Combs-la-Ville, and applied for a patent for a glass-molding process. In 1912 he held the last exhibition of his jewelry in the shop in the place Vendôme. He went on to become a pioneer in modern glass design and production and one of the masters of the Art Deco style. The Musée des arts décoratifs in Paris organized the first retrospective exhibition of his work in 1933.

Lawrence, F. Walter

1864–1929

Influential American jeweler and silver designer. He apprenticed with the jewelry manufacturer Durand and Company in Newark, New Jersey, and is also thought to have apprenticed with the silver firm Howard and Company and with the jewelers Jaques and Marcus, both in New York City. In 1889 he established his first business at 12 Centre Street, Newark, moving to 857 Broadway, New York City, in 1894. In 1898 he opened an upstairs jewelry salon at 41 Union Square, where he catered to a select clientele (it moved to 322 Fifth Avenue in 1905 and to 527 Fifth Avenue in 1915). His designs were inspired primarily by nature, but he also designed pieces incorporating Egyptian motifs, mermaids, and mythological figures such as Psyche. Lawrence was fond of unusual stones, and around 1903 he created jewelry (including cat. 53) featuring baroque pearls or fragments of ancient Cyprian or Phoenician glass, in which the ideas for the designs were taken from the shape and character of the materials. In 1903 he exhibited these pieces at Arts and Crafts exhibitions in New York City, Syracuse, and Rochester, New York, and published articles explaining them in *Town and Country* and *The Craftsman*. At the Louisiana Purchase Exposition in Saint Louis in 1904, Lawrence exhibited twenty-seven pieces of jewelry, many of them made for him by the New York jeweler Gustav Manz; he continued to exhibit at Arts and Crafts exhibitions for the remainder of his career. Around 1900 he began to offer silver wares in his salon, and by 1920 he was designing his own pieces, which were made for him by Lebkuecher and Company of Newark. After Lawrence's death in 1929, his company (which had been incorporated in 1913) continued, under the direction of various family members, to offer handcrafted jewelry and silverware, until it was finally dissolved in 1975.

Liénard, Paul
1849–?

French jeweler, student of designer Eugène Grasset and sculptor Théophile Barrau. His maker's mark was registered in 1905, but his designs and jewels had appeared in the press in 1902 and 1903, and he is known to have designed a buckle for the Saint Petersburg jeweler Bolin in 1901. Liénard's workshop in Paris was located first at 7, rue Joubert, then at 49, rue Cambon in 1906, and at 18, rue du Faubourg Saint-Honoré in 1908. He showed his work at the Salon des artistes décorateurs in 1906 and at the Salon des artistes français between 1907 and 1910. His Art Nouveau jewels, many featuring seaweed motifs or cascading clusters of baroque pearls, were much admired for their elegance and graceful naturalism. He also designed a border of seaweed motifs for the jewelry magazine *La revue de la bijouterie, joaillerie, orfèvrerie.*

Louchet

French firm founded by Paul Louchet (1854–1936), a jeweler, sculptor, and bronze caster. Much of Paul Louchet's work was created together with his brother Albert and exhibited under the name Paul-Albert Louchet. The names and biographical details of the two brothers have become confused, but Paul is thought to have studied painting with Henri-Joseph Harpignies and Jules Lefebvre or Paul Lecomte before turning to sculpture, and one of the brothers is thought to have studied at the Ecole des arts décoratifs. The brothers set up a workshop and foundry at 20, rue Notre-Dame-de-Nazareth, Paris, where they cast their own sculptures and edited those of many other sculptors. They also produced jewelry, *cloisonné* enameled objects (for which they may have employed Japanese enamelers), and furniture, and collaborated with other artists on mixed-media sculptures in glass or ceramic with bronze. At some point, one or both of the brothers had a shop or workshop at 3, rue Auber (this address

appears on the original box for cat. 44). They exhibited jewelry, metalwork, and *cloisonné* enamels at the Salon des artistes français between 1902 and 1908 and at the Salon du mobilier in 1905. In 1909 Paul Louchet registered his maker's mark and gave his workshop address as 8, rue Boudreau; the mark was registered until 1920.

Rambour, André

French jeweler. His maker's mark was registered between 1891 and 1906, and the address of his workshop was listed as 43, rue de Turbigo. Included by Henri Vever among those "who have created charming jewelry of modern inspiration," his firm exhibited Art Nouveau jewelry at the 1900 Exposition universelle and the 1903 Salon des artistes français.

Riker Brothers

American jewelry firm active in Newark, New Jersey, between 1892 and 1926. William Riker (1822–1898) apprenticed with jewelers in New York City before opening his first shop, Riker and Tay, in Newark in 1846. Around 1849 he entered into a new partnership, Riker and Goble; he then ran the business under his own name from 1864 until the 1870s, when he was joined by his sons, William Jr., Joseph M., and Cortland. The firm was renamed Riker and Sons and relocated to 42 Court Street. In 1892 William Sr. and Cortland withdrew from the business, which was renamed Riker Brothers. Early on, William Riker Jr. manufactured Masonic goods and made gold fob chains and charms. The range of the company expanded through the 1870s and 1880s, and by the end of the century it was producing a full line of high-quality jewelry and was one of the few Newark firms using *plique à jour* enamel. Less is known about the later history of the firm, but it exhibited at the 1916 Newark Industrial Exposition, and its factory appeared in city directories until 1926.

Rothmüller, Karl
1860–1930

German jeweler and goldsmith; the most prominent of a group of Munich jewelers creating a distinctive kind of jewelry in the Art Nouveau style (called *Jugendstil* in German) around 1900. He studied at the Applied Arts Academies in Munich and Vienna and with jewelers in Berlin, Paris, and London, and from 1883 to 1885 he was a student of Fritz von Miller in Munich. In 1886 he founded his own workshop. At first he worked in a Neo-Renaissance style, but in the 1890s he turned to designs based on natural forms and Symbolist imagery. Rothmüller was influenced by the organization and symmetry found in the plates of biologist Ernst Haeckel's book *Kunstformen der Natur* (Art Forms of Nature) and used carefully chosen colored stones to suggest natural structures and patterns. He also made frequent use of baroque pearls. He exhibited at the 1900 Exposition universelle, receiving a silver medal. After 1922 Rothmüller worked with his sons Karl and Hanns, and in 1925 he was named a professor at the Applied Arts Academy in Munich.

Roty, Louis Oscar
1846–1911

French sculptor and medalist. Roty was a leading figure in the revival of the art of the medal and was considered the first to realize its potential in jewelry. He studied with Auguste Dumont and Hubert Ponscarme at the Ecole des beaux-arts in Paris and exhibited at the Salon des artistes français, receiving a third-class medal in 1873, the Prix de Rome in 1875, a second-class medal in 1882, a first-class medal in 1885, and a medal of honor in 1905. For the 1889 Exposition universelle, he created a "centenary" bracelet (to mark the centenary of the French Revolution) for the jeweler Charles Rivaud and received a grand prix. In the 1890s he was commissioned by another jeweler, Germain Desbazeille, to make plaques and medals for jewelry, and he also provided them to numerous others (including Comte Enguerrand du Suau de la Croix—see cat. 69). Roty was appointed professor and, in 1897, president of the Académie des beaux-arts, and he received another grand prix at the 1900 Exposition universelle. He designed the figure of the *Semeuse* (the Sower), which has appeared on many French coins and stamps.

Sandoz, Gustave-Roger
1867-?
French jeweler, son of watchmaker and jeweler Gustave Sandoz, who was himself the son of a Swiss watchmaker. Gustave started out as a watchmaker, but in 1865 he moved his shop to the Palais-Royal and began to make jewelry as well. He was active in professional societies and exhibited and served on the jury for the 1878 and 1889 Expositions universelles. Upon his death in 1891, he was succeeded by his son Gustave-Roger, who increasingly specialized in gem-set jewelry. Gustave-Roger opened a second shop at 10, rue Royale in 1895. He was on the jury for the 1900 Exposition universelle, where his display, including a wide variety of jewelry along with decorative objects, "dazzlingly sustained his firm's reputation" and "attracted a great deal of attention," according to Henri Vever. Sandoz also exhibited his Art Nouveau-style jewelry, in both enameled gold and gold set with diamonds, at the 1904 Salon des artistes français and in the French section of the 1902 Glasgow International Exposition. His son Gérard (1902-1995) began to design for his father in the 1920s and became one of the most important creators of Art Deco jewelry. He took over the firm after his father's retirement, but closed it in 1931 to concentrate on painting and the cinema.

Soloviev, Vladimir
Russian goldsmith, workmaster for Fabergé. He took over the workshop of Philip Theodor Ringe, who had overseen it since 1893, after Ringe's death (date unknown). This workshop made jewelry, along with objects in enameled gold and silver such as cigarette cases and paper knives. Soloviev's initials in the Cyrillic alphabet, B. C., often appear on enameled objects made for export to England, suggesting a date after Fabergé's London branch opened in 1903.

Suau de la Croix, Comte Enguerrand du
French jeweler and enameler, best known for his mastery of *cabochonné* enameling, a variation of *plique à jour* enameling in which cells of enamel are built up in high relief, imitating cabochon stones. His work was often inspired by medieval or Renaissance ornament, and many of his pieces incorporate medals, plaques, or portrait miniatures, with the enamel acting as a "jeweled" frame. He exhibited his work at the Salon des artistes français between about 1899 and 1908, receiving an honorable mention in 1899 and a third-class medal in 1902. He also exhibited at the 1907 Salon des beaux-arts and the 1908 Exposition de la parure précieuse de la femme. His pupil Jeanne de Montigny was one of the few other jewelers to use the *cabochonné* technique.

Vever, Paul and Henri
1850-1915 and 1854-1942
French jewelers; partners in the firm of Vever, a leading exponent of Art Nouveau jewelry. Henri was also the author of *La bijouterie française au XIXe siècle* (*French Jewelry of the Nineteenth Century*), an indispensable reference work first published in 1906–8. Paul and Henri were the sons of jeweler Ernest Vever, who in 1870 moved from Metz to Paris and bought into the firm of Baugrand at 19, rue de la Paix. Ernest Vever exhibited at and was a member of the jury for

the 1878 Exposition universelle. His sons joined his workshop in 1874 and took over the firm in 1881; Paul took over the commercial and administrative side of the business, and Henri the artistic and technical side. Within a few years, Vever was considered one of the leading jewelers in Paris, renowned for both gem-set jewelry and enameled gold pieces, and its display received a grand prix at the 1889 Exposition universelle. In addition to Henri's own designs, the brothers commissioned jewelry from other designers and makers, including Jules Brateau, Léopold Gautrait, and René Lalique. During the 1890s, perhaps following the example of Lalique, Vever turned to a more naturalistic style and received another grand prix, at the 1897 Brussels International Exhibition. For the 1900 Exposition universelle, the firm commissioned a group of twenty Symbolist jewels from designer Eugène Grasset, and Henri Vever created a group of dramatic and original Art Nouveau diadems set with diamonds; Vever's display was considered exceptional for both the number and the quality of works displayed and again received a grand prix. In 1908 the company moved to 14, rue de la Paix. After Paul's death in 1915, Henri became the sole director, but business declined during World War I, and in 1921 Henri handed over the firm to his nephews André and Pierre. They continued to run the business until 1960; Jean Vever, who had joined them in 1934, ran it from 1960 until it closed in 1982.

Wolfers, Philippe
1858-1929
Belgian jeweler, sculptor, and gold- and silversmith; one of the leading creators of Art Nouveau jewelry. He was the son of goldsmith Louis Wolfers (1820-1892) and heir to the family firm of court jewelers, Wolfers frères, founded in Brussels in 1812. Philippe Wolfers studied sculpture at the Académie royale des beaux-arts in Brussels before starting as an apprentice at Wolfers frères. As part

of his work for the firm, he frequently traveled to visit clients in France, Germany, and Holland and attended the various international exhibitions, where he was introduced to Asian art. He began to design silverware and jewelry around 1880; at first he worked in a Rococo-revival style, but toward 1890 his work began to show the influence of Japanese art and naturalism. In 1892, after his father's death, he became artistic director of Wolfers frères, thereafter designing silver and jewelry for the firm in both Art Nouveau and conventional styles. (His brothers, Max and Robert, together with their cousin Albert, were his collaborators in the firm and played important roles in expanding its business.) In the same year, he was one of the artists selected by the Belgian government to work with the first elephant ivory from the Belgian Congo. He is thought to have set up a private workshop in 1893 in the Square Marie-Louise, with five specialized craftsmen, to produce a collection of Art Nouveau jewelry and small decorative objects, which he presented as distinct from his work for the family firm. (There may also have been a workshop at the Art Nouveau-style villa that he built at La Hulpe in 1899.) Between 1894 and 1904, Wolfers created a series of unique Art Nouveau pieces, each of which (including cats. 67 and 38) was marked with his monogram and the inscription "ex unique"–for *examplaire unique* (unique example). These splendid and personal creations, inspired by the natural world and by Symbolist imagery, combined gold, carved stones, and pearls with *plique à jour* enamel, which Wolfers had learned from the eminent French enameler Louis Houillon. They were widely published and exhibited at numerous international expositions, including those of Munich in 1898 and 1899, Brussels in 1897, Turin in 1902, and Milan in 1906. During the 1900 Exposition universelle, they were shown in the galerie Aublanc. They also did much to strengthen the artistic reputation of Wolfers

Fig. 33
Murakami Jochiku (Japanese, died about 1790–1800), *Tsuba with design of dragonfly and suisen (narcissus),* late 18th–early 19th century, *shakudō*, gold, *shibuichi,* and shell

frères, which participated in the same exhibitions. (Recent research suggests that this may, in fact, have been Philippe Wolfers' primary intent in creating them.) Although Wolfers' output was quite small, his work was greatly admired, with many contemporary critics considering him the one artist whose jewelry was on a par with that of René Lalique. Around 1905 Wolfers began to turn his attention to sculpture, though he continued to design for Wolfers frères. In the 1920s he modernized the firm's designs, and in 1925 he designed a critically acclaimed dining room interior for the Belgian Pavilion at the Exposition des arts decoratifs. Philippe's son, Marcel (1886–1976), also designed for the family firm but was better known for his sculpture and lacquerwork.

Zorra, Louis

Jeweler working in Paris in the early twentieth century. He registered his maker's mark in 1901, and his workshop was located at 30, rue Volta. According to Victor Arwas's book *Art Nouveau: The French Aesthetic* (London: Andreas Papadakis, 2002), he moved to Paris from Asti, Italy, and exhibited at the Salon des artistes français, receiving an honorable mention in 1902.

CHECKLIST AND FIGURE ILLUSTRATIONS

Note to the reader

Unless otherwise noted, all pieces of jewelry are from a single private collection, and their dimensions are given as height by width by depth.

The maker's marks are described as completely as possible. The most easily recognized and commonly seen French mark is the eagle's head, which has been in use since 1838. An assay or guarantee mark, it indicates that the object is made of 18-karat gold. It was also around 1838 that the French government required a maker's mark in the form of an impressed diamond for gold, silver, and platinum objects. Within the diamond are the maker's initials, separated by a symbol unique to the maker. In the United States, assay marks were not required on jewelry until 1906. For gold items, the karat (abbreviated *Kt* or *K*) was used as a measure of fineness: 24 karat is pure gold, 18 karat is 18/24 gold, and 14 karat is 14/24 gold.

1
René Lalique
French, 1860–1945
Carnation brooch, 1900–1902
Gold, enamel, opal, and cast glass
5.7 x 6.6 x 2.2 cm (2¼ x 2⅝ x ⅞ in.)
Marks: *LALIQUE* on both edges of left outer bud; owls on pin catch and pin stem

2
René Lalique
French, 1860–1945
Pendant-brooch with pink carnations, 1901–2
Gold, enamel, pink sapphire, and cast glass
8.1 x 6.6 x 1.6 cm (3³⁄₁₆ x 2⅝ x ⅝ in.)
Marks: *LALIQUE* on top outer edge and under branch

3
René Lalique
French, 1860–1945
Floral brooch, 1901–2
Gold, enamel, diamond, and cast glass
5.5 x 8.8 x 1.9 cm (2³⁄₁₆ x 3⁷⁄₁₆ x ¾ in.)
Marks: *LALIQUE* on lower-right bottom edge; eagle's head on armature

4
René Lalique
French, 1860–1945
Side element of a corsage ornament with pinecones, 1900–1902
Gold, enamel, and cast glass
5.2 x 1.2 x 7 cm (2¹⁄₁₆ x ½ x 2¾ in.)
Marks: None

5
René Lalique
French, 1860–1945
Hair comb with ivy leaves, 1902–3
Gold, enamel, sapphire, and horn
17.2 x 8 x 0.6 cm (6¾ x 3⅛ x ¼ in.)
Marks: *LALIQUE* on bezel of second sapphire from left

6
René Lalique
French, 1860–1945
Carnation watch, 1898–1900
Gold, enamel, and crystal
7.8 x 5.4 x 1.1 cm (3¹⁄₁₆ x 2⅛ x ⁷⁄₁₆ in.)
Marks: *LALIQUE* on bottom left of case; owls on watch stem and inside case; rows of ants on watch stem; engraved *17382* on inside case, covering the works

7
René Lalique
French, 1860–1945
Dog collar plaque with a floral motif, 1899–1901
Gold, enamel, and diamond
5 x 7.7 x 2.3 cm (1¹⁵⁄₁₆ x 3¹⁄₁₆ x ⅞ in.)
Marks: *LALIQUE* on bottom of frame

8
René Lalique
French, 1860–1945
Branch brooch with cherry blossoms, 1900–1902
Gold, diamond, and cast glass
3.3 x 14.3 x 1.3 cm (1⁵⁄₁₆ x 5⅝ x ½ in.)
Marks: *LALIQUE* on outer edge

9
René Lalique
French, 1860–1945
Vine and berries hair comb, about 1900
Gold and ivory
10.8 x 11.3 x 2 cm (4¼ x 4⁷⁄₁₆ x ¹³⁄₁₆ in.)
Marks: *LALIQUE* on reverse

10
René Lalique
French, 1860–1945
Fringe necklace with blister pearls, about 1902–3
Gold, enamel, and pearl
Necklace: 37 cm (14⁹⁄₁₆ in.) long
Pendants: 4.6 x 1.6 x 0.6 cm (1¹³⁄₁₆ x ⅝ x ¼ in.) each
Marks: *LALIQUE* on side of several pendants; two eagles' heads on jump ring

11
René Lalique
French, 1860–1945
Thistle necklace, 1904–5
Gold, enamel, diamond, pearl, and cast glass
4.3 x 1.1 x 43 cm (1¹¹⁄₁₆ x ⁷⁄₁₆ x 16⅛ in.)
Marks: *LALIQUE* on outer edge of each element; owl on spring ring

12
René Lalique
French, 1860–1945
Belt buckle, about 1900
Gold, enamel, and opal
5.8 x 8.2 x 0.6 cm (2 5/16 x 3 1/4 x 1/4 in.)
Marks: *LALIQUE* on reverse on tine

13
René Lalique
French, 1860–1945
Flowering tree brooch, about 1910
Steel
4.4 x 8.2 x 1.2 cm (1 3/4 x 3 1/4 x 1/2 in.)
Marks: *LALIQUE* on reverse on bottom left

14
René Lalique
French, 1860–1945
Dog collar plaques with carnations,
1899–1900
Gold, enamel, diamond, pearl, and topaz
5.6 x 4.5 x 1.3 cm (2 3/16 x 1 3/4 x 1/2 in.)
Marks: None remaining, because of
alterations

15
René Lalique
French, 1860–1945
Box with olive tree motif, about 1900
Gold, enamel, and smoky quartz
3.3 x 5.8 cm (1 5/16 x 2 5/16 in.)
Marks: *LALIQUE* on outer edge of rim

16
René Lalique
French, 1860–1945
Pendant-brooch with a village scene, about
1900
Platinum, gold, enamel, and diamond
4.4 x 4.5 x 0.9 cm (1 3/4 x 1 3/4 x 3/8 in.)
Marks: Impressed diamond with the initials
R and *L* separated by a hammer along bottom
edge; stamped *MD* along bottom edge; eagle's
head on pin stem

17
René Lalique
French, 1860–1945
Lily-of-the-valley necklace, about 1920
Gold and cast glass
Necklace: 46.7 cm (18 3/8 in.) long
Pendant: 14.8 x 5 x 0.8 cm (5 13/16 x 1 15/16 x 5/16 in.)
Marks: *LALIQUE* on lower left pendant and
upper right pendant; eagle's head on clasp

18
Louis Zorra
Possibly born in Italy, working in Paris
Brooch with an opal and pearl, about 1900
Gold, silver, enamel, sapphire, opal, and
pearl
5.3 x 4.9 x 1.4 cm (2 1/16 x 1 15/16 x 9/16 in.)
Marks: Impressed diamond with illegible ini-
tials separated by a crown; eagle's head on
front lower vine

19
Lucien Gaillard
French, 1861–1933
Necklace with bleeding hearts, about 1907
Gold and enamel
3.4 x 0.4 x 43.8 cm (1 5/16 x 3/16 x 17 1/4 in.)
Marks: *L. GAILLARD* and impressed diamond
with the letters *L* and *G* separated by two
crossed hammers; eagle's head behind central
element

20
Designed by Charles Desrosiers
French
For Georges Fouquet, French, 1862–1957
Orchid brooch, 1898–1901
Gold, enamel, diamond, and pearl
8.5 x 11.3 x 2 cm (3 3/8 x 4 7/16 x 13/16 in.)
Marks: *G. Fouquet* on riveting mechanism;
eagle's head on pin stem

21
Designed by Charles Desrosiers
French
For Georges Fouquet, French, 1862–1957
Brooch with leaves and blossoms, 1901
Gold, enamel, diamond, and baroque pearl

7.4 x 11 x 2.1 cm (2 15/16 x 4 5/16 x 13/16 in.)
Marks: *G Fouquet* on reverse; impressed
diamond with the initials *G* and *F* separated
by a whip; two eagles' heads on top right edge

22
Paul Liénard
French, 1849–?
Seaweed brooch, about 1908
Gold and mabe pearl
5.4 x 11 x 1 cm (2 1/8 x 4 5/16 x 3/8 in.)
Marks: Two impressed diamonds with the
initials *P* and *L* separated by a leaf on reverse
at the tips of the marquis-shaped elements;
eagles' heads on pin stem and next to one of
the maker's marks
Museum of Fine Arts, Boston. Gift of Joe and
Ruth Sataloff in honor of Susan B. Kaplan
2007.892

23
Unknown maker
Possibly Austrian
Ivy brooch, about 1900
Platinum, gold, enamel, diamond, and peridot
5.1 x 13.7 x 2.1 cm (2 x 5 3/8 x 13/16 in.)
Marks: Owl and impressed head of a bearded
man at bottom of left berry; owl with the
number *75* on pin stem

24
Unknown maker
American
Orchid pendant, about 1905
Gold, enamel, diamond, and pearl
6.2 x 3.3 x 1.1 cm (2 7/16 x 1 5/16 x 7/16 in.)
Marks: None
Museum of Fine Arts, Boston. Gift of Dr. and
Mrs. Joseph Sataloff   2007.635

25
Paul-Emile Brandt
French, 1883–1952
*Pendant necklace with butterflies and blos-
soms*, about 1911
Platinum, gold, enamel, diamond, and opal
Necklace: 30.2 cm (11 7/8 in.) long
Pendant: 7.3 x 5.3 x 0.7 cm (2 7/8 x 2 1/16 x 1/4 in.)

Marks: *P. BRANDT 1013* on bottom edge of reverse; impressed diamond with the initials *P* and *B* separated by a torch on the chain; eagle's head on hoop of chain

26
KARL ROTHMÜLLER
German, 1860-1930
Pendant necklace, about 1910
Gold, silver, enamel, green stone, red stone, and pearl
Necklace: 44.6 cm (17 9/16 in.) long
Pendant: 5.3 x 3.4 x 0.4 cm (2 1/16 x 1 5/16 x 3/16 in.)
Marks: None; *Rothmüller/K.B. Hofgoldschmed/MUNCHEN* stamped in gold on silk inside fitted box

27
UNKNOWN MAKER
French
Pendant-brooch with leaves and berries, about 1900
Gold, enamel, diamond, and tourmaline
9 x 7 x 1.4 cm (3 9/16 x 2 3/4 x 9/16 in.)
Marks: Eagle's head on pin stem

28
LÉOPOLD ALBERT MARIN GAUTRAIT
French, 1865-1937
For LÉON GARIOD, French
Pendant necklace with carnations, 1904
Gold, enamel, and diamond
Necklace: 32.4 cm (12 3/4 in.) long
Pendant: 9 x 5.4 x 2.2 cm (3 9/16 x 2 1/8 x 7/8 in.)
Marks: *L. GAUTRAIT* on reverse on lower edge; impressed diamond with the initials *L* and *G* separated by a horn and an eagle's head on spring ring

29
UNKNOWN MAKER
French
Brooch with bamboo stalks and leaves, about 1900
Gold, enamel, opal, and glass
5 x 5.7 x 1.2 cm (1 15/16 x 2 1/4 x 1/2 in.)
Marks: Impressed diamond with the letters *Y* and *D* separated by an ankh above pin-stem

hinge; eagle's head above tip of pin stem; illegible mark on pin stem

30
FUSET GRAU
Probably Spanish
Bracelet with scrolls and leaves, about 1900
Platinum, gold, diamond, and citrine
3.2 x 6.9 x 6.6 cm (1 1/4 x 2 11/16 x 2 5/8 in.)
Marks: *FUSET GRAU* on applied tab on side of bezel

31
HENRI VEVER
French, 1854-1942
Belt buckle with lily pads and blossoms, about 1900
Gold, enamel, and diamond
8 x 5.2 x 1.2 cm (3 1/8 x 2 1/16 x 1/2 in.)
Marks: *VEVER PARIS* on bottom edge; impressed ants and eagle's head on hinge; *1210* and two illegible marks on bottom of reverse

32
FRANK GARDNER HALE
American, 1876-1945
Pendant, about 1910
Gold, diamond, and green tourmaline
7.3 x 4.1 x 0.6 cm (2 7/8 x 1 5/8 x 1/4 in.)
Marks: *F.G. Hale* on applied tab on left shoulder of reverse
Museum of Fine Arts, Boston. Anonymous promised gift

33
Possibly by EMMANUEL-JULES-JOSEPH (JOË) DESCOMPS
French, 1872-1948
Pendant with blossoms, about 1900
Gold, enamel, and emerald
12.5 x 4.7 x 0.7 cm (4 15/16 x 1 7/8 x 1/4 in.)
Marks: Impressed diamond with the initials *J* and *D* separated by an illegible symbol on bail; four eagles' heads: one on front near pendant drop, one on bail, and two adjacent to bail

34
RENÉ LALIQUE
French, 1860-1945
For HENRI VEVER, French, 1854-1942, and PAUL VEVER, French, 1850-1915
Swallow brooch, 1889
Gold, silver, enamel, diamond, and ruby
6.9 x 11.7 x 2.4 cm (2 11/16 x 4 5/8 x 15/16 in.)
Marks: *VEVER* on inner tip of left wing; eagle's head on outer tip of left wing; *6412* on right wing; impressed diamond with the initials *R* and *L* on outer tip of right wing

35
RENÉ LALIQUE
French, 1860-1945
Hair ornament with antennae, about 1900
Gold, silver, steel, and diamond
8.8 x 12.5 x 7 cm (3 7/16 x 4 15/16 x 2 3/4 in.)
Marks: Impressed diamond with the initials *R* and *L* separated by a sword on top of left arm of loop; eagle's head on top of right arm

36
RENÉ LALIQUE
French, 1860-1945
Pendant-brooch with wasps, about 1900
Gold, enamel, diamond, emerald, ruby, sapphire, and opal
4.1 x 6.2 x 1 cm (1 5/8 x 2 7/16 x 3/8 in.)
Marks: *LALIQUE* on underside; eagle's head on bottom edge

37
RENÉ LALIQUE
French, 1860-1945
Brooch with rooster, 1898-1900
Gold and enamel
5.8 x 7.9 x 0.7 cm (2 5/16 x 3 1/8 x 1/4 in.)
Marks: *LALIQUE* on bottom left edge; eagle's head on pin stem

38
PHILIPPE WOLFERS
Belgian, 1858-1929
"Dragonfly" pendant-brooch, 1904
Platinum, gold, enamel, diamond, ruby, and pearl

7.2 x 11.9 x 2 cm (2¹³⁄₁₆ x 4¹¹⁄₁₆ x ¹³⁄₁₆ in.)
Marks: *WP EX UNIQUE* on reverse

39
UNKNOWN MAKER
French
Moth brooch, about 1900
Gold, enamel, diamond, and pearl
3.8 x 7.4 x 1.1 cm (1½ x 2¹⁵⁄₁₆ x ⁷⁄₁₆ in.)
Marks: Eagle's head on reverse

40
UNKNOWN MAKER
Probably American
En tremblant dragonfly brooch, about 1900
Platinum, gold, enamel, diamond, emerald,
and ruby
4.7 x 9.2 x 1.7 cm (1⅞ x 3⅝ x ¹¹⁄₁₆ in.)
Marks: None

41
Probably by LOUIS AUCOC
French, 1850–1932
Butterfly brooch, about 1900
Platinum, gold, enamel, emerald, ruby,
sapphire, and horn
6.2 x 9.7 x 1.5 cm (2⁷⁄₁₆ x 3¹³⁄₁₆ x ⁹⁄₁₆ in.)
Marks: Impressed diamond with illegible
marks; eagle's head on pin stem

42
LOUIS AUCOC
French, 1850–1932
Dragonfly brooch, about 1900
Platinum, gold, enamel, diamond, emerald,
ruby, and horn
6.7 x 12.6 x 1.2 cm (2⅝ x 4¹⁵⁄₁₆ x ½ in.)
Marks: Impressed diamond with the initials
L and *A* separated by a wolf facing left on pin
stem; eagle's head and *6282* on insect's leg

43
LÉOPOLD ALBERT MARIN GAUTRAIT
French, 1865–1937
For LÉON GARIOD, French
Pendant necklace with two swans, about
1900
Gold, enamel, diamond, pearl, and peridot

Necklace: 34.5 cm (13⁹⁄₁₆ in.) long
Pendant: 8.3 x 5.2 x 0.5 cm (3¼ x 2¹⁄₁₆ x ³⁄₁₆ in.)
Marks: Impressed diamond with the initials
L and *G* and an illegible symbol on spring
ring; eagle's head on right side of reverse

44
VICTOR GÉRARD
French
Retailed by LOUCHET, French
Pendant necklace with swallows, about 1900
Gold and enamel
Necklace: 40.1 cm (15¹³⁄₁₆ in.) long
Pendant: 10.4 x 6.9 x 0.6 cm (4⅛ x 2¹¹⁄₁₆ x ¼ in.)
Marks: Impressed diamond with the initials
V and *G* separated by two crossed hammers
and an eagle's head on tang of clasp;
Louchet/Ciseleur/3, Rue Auber/PARIS
stamped in gold on silk inside fitted box

45
VICTOR GÉRARD
French
Peacock necklace, about 1900
Gold, enamel, and pearl
Necklace: 56.4 cm (22³⁄₁₆ in.) long
Pendant: 6.5 x 4.8 x 1.2 cm (2⁹⁄₁₆ x 1⅞ x ½ in.)
Marks: Impressed diamond with the initials
V and *G* separated by two crossed hammers;
eagle's head on left edge

46
EUGÈNE FEUILLÂTRE
French, 1870–1916
Double peacock necklace, about 1900
Gold, enamel, diamond, and opal
Necklace: 50 cm (19¹¹⁄₁₆ in.) long
Pendant: 4.3 x 7.3 x 0.5 cm (1¹¹⁄₁₆ x 2⅞ x
³⁄₁₆ in.)
Marks: *FEUILLATRE* on right bottom edge;
eagle's head on right edge

47
GEORGES FOUQUET
French, 1862–1957
Belt buckle with two peacocks, about 1900
Gold and enamel
Necklace: 74.8 cm (29⁷⁄₁₆ in.) long

Pendant: 7.4 x 5.1 x 1.5 cm (2¹⁵⁄₁₆ x 2 x ⁹⁄₁₆ in.)
Marks: Engraved *G. Fouquet* and *3183* on
reverse; eagle's head on reverse along bottom
edge

48
LUCIEN GAILLARD
French, 1861–1933
Beetle necklace, about 1900
Gold, patinated silver, enamel, diamond,
and pearl
Necklace: 51.7 cm (20⅜ in.) long
Pendant: 12.5 x 7.1 x 1.6 cm (4¹⁵⁄₁₆ x 2¹³⁄₁₆ x ⅝ in.)
Marks: *L. GAILLARD* and two unidentified
impressed marks on right leg of beetle;
impressed *HR* on left leg; stamped *925* on
right joint; dolphins on jump ring

49
MAURICE-PHILIPPE FOURAIN
French
*Pendant necklace with two intertwined
serpents*, 1911
Gold, silver, aquamarine, and ivory
Necklace: 34 cm (13⅜ in.) long
Pendant: 11 x 9.2 x 0.7 cm (4⁵⁄₁₆ x 3⅝ x ¼ in.)
Marks: *MAURICE P. FOURAIN MARS 1911 RHEIMS*
on reverse; impressed boar's head on clasp

50
GUSTAVE-ROGER SANDOZ
French, 1867–?
*Pendant-brooch with a pond scene and two
swans*, about 1900
Gold and enamel
4.7 x 6.5 x 1.2 cm (1⅞ x 2⁹⁄₁₆ x ½ in.)
Marks: Impressed diamond with the initials
G and *R* with an illegible symbol on pin stem;
engraved *G-R Sandoz* on reverse; eagle's head
on pin stem

51
LUCIEN HIRTZ
French, 1864–1928
Probably made by GUSTAVE ESPINASSE, French
Gem carved by BURDY, French
For FRÉDÉRIC BOUCHERON, French, 1830–1902
Belt buckle with lionesses, 1900

Gold, emerald, and garnet
7.8 x 5.8 x 1.7 cm (3¹/₁₆ x 2⁵/₁₆ x ¹¹/₁₆ in.)
Marks: *F. BOUCHERON/PARIS* on reverse;
eagle's head on underside of buckle;
impressed diamond with the initials *G* and *E*
separated by an ace of clubs on reverse;
impressed ants on reverse

52
UNKNOWN MAKER
French
Egyptian-revival tiara comb and bracelet,
about 1900
Gold, enamel, ruby, sapphire, and glazed
steatite (ancient Egyptian scarabs)
Tiara comb: 9.7 x 9.2 x 1.1 cm (3¹³/₁₆ x 3⁵/₈ x
⁷/₁₆ in.)
Bracelet: 2.5 x 7.5 x 1 cm (1¹/₈ x 6¾ x ¾ in.)
Marks: Impressed diamond with an illegible
letter and a *V* separated by an illegible sym-
bol, next to two eagles' heads, on bottom gold
rim of tiara comb

53
F. WALTER LAWRENCE
American, 1864-1929
Dog collar with a nautical scene, about 1903
Gold and pearl
3.9 x 2.3 x 31 cm (1⁹/₁₆ x ⁷/₈ x 12³/₁₆ in.)
Marks: None; *F. Walter Lawrence/41 Union
Square/NEW YORK* stamped in gold on satin
inside original leather box

54
UNKNOWN MAKER
American
Hair comb with a profile dragon on a wave,
about 1910
Gold, emerald, ruby, pearl, and horn
11.5 x 4 x 0.7 cm (4½ x 1⁹/₁₆ x ¼ in.)
Marks: None
Museum of Fine Arts, Boston. Gift of Dr. and
Mrs. Joseph Sataloff   2007.638

55
RENÉ LALIQUE
French, 1860-1945
Pendant necklace with a figure of Flora,
1904-5
Gold, opal, and *pâte de verre* glass
Necklace: 29.7 cm (11¹¹/₁₆ in.) long
Pendant: 6.3 x 3.8 x 0.5 cm (2½ x 1½ x ³/₁₆ in.)
Marks: *LALIQUE* on left shoulder; eagle's head
on jump ring of chain

56
RENÉ LALIQUE
French, 1860-1945
Pendant necklace with three female figures,
1904-5
Gold, peridot, and engraved glass
Pendant: 5.8 x 4.3 x 0.3 cm (2⁵/₁₆ x 1¹¹/₁₆ x
⅛ in.)
Marks: *LALIQUE* on left outer edge

57
RENÉ LALIQUE
French, 1860-1945
Brooch with a female figure, about 1903
Gold, enamel, and diamond
3.8 x 6.9 x 1 cm (1½ x 2¹¹/₁₆ x ⅜ in)
Marks: *LALIQUE* on middle-bottom edge;
eagle's head on pin stem

58
RENÉ LALIQUE
French, 1860-1945
*Brooch with dancing nymphs in butterfly
frame*, 1901-2
Gold, enamel, sapphire, and cast glass
4.8 x 6 x 0.6 cm (1⅞ x 2⅜ x ¼ in.)
Marks: *LALIQUE* on bottom edge

59
RENÉ LALIQUE
French, 1860-1945
Hair comb with female figures and thistles,
about 1901-2
Silver, horn, and *pâte de verre* glass
9.8 x 10.5 x 2.5 cm (3⅞ x 4⅛ x 1 in.)
Marks: *LALIQUE* on reverse of horn

60
RENÉ LALIQUE
French, 1860-1945
Pendant with wood nymph, 1904-5
Gold, enamel, and artificial ivory
7 x 8.4 x 0.4 cm (2¾ x 3⁵/₁₆ x ³/₁₆ in.)
Marks: *LALIQUE* on bottom edge of frame

61
RENÉ LALIQUE
French, 1860-1945
Handle with sweet pea and a female bust,
1899-1900
Gold, enamel, and cast glass
10.5 x 5.3 x 5.4 cm (4⅛ x 2¹/₁₆ x 2⅛ in.)
Marks: *LALIQUE* on right edge of blossom;
impressed diamond with the initials *R* and *L*
on upper hoop; eagle's head on upper hoop;
14K on right shoulder of handle (later addition)

62
Probably by LOUIS AUCOC
French, 1850-1932
Pendant-brooch with a female bust,
about 1900
Gold, enamel, and pearl
5.6 x 4.9 x 1 cm (2³/₁₆ x 1¹⁵/₁₆ x ⅜ in.)
Marks: Partial impressed diamond with the
initial *A* and a wolf facing left on pin catch;
eagle's head on pin catch; two owls with
illegible numbers at top of head

63
ANDRÉ RAMBOUR
French
Pendant with a water scene and two figures,
about 1900
Gold and enamel
5.9 x 4.8 x 0.6 cm (2⁵/₁₆ x 1⅞ x ¼ in.)
Marks: Impressed diamond on reverse with
the initials *A* and *R* separated by an apple;
eagle's head on bail

64
UNKNOWN MAKER
Probably French
Pendant with a female head in a sheep frame,
about 1900

Gold, diamond, and pearl
10.7 x 3.7 x 0.7 cm (4³⁄₁₆ x 1⁷⁄₁₆ x ¼ in.)
Marks: None

Mold for the pendant, about 1900
Wood
3.4 x 3.6 x 0.3 cm (1⁵⁄₁₆ x 1⁷⁄₁₆ x ⅛ in.)
Marks: None

65
EDMOND-HENRI BECKER, relief plaque
French, 1871-?
LOUIS AUCOC, frame
French, 1850-1932
Brooch with children in a floral frame, 1899
Gold and enamel
3.5 x 5.8 x 0.9 cm (1⅜ x 2⁵⁄₁₆ x ⅜ in.)
Marks: Partial eagle's head and diamond with
an illegible impressed mark on pin catch; an
eagle's head on bottom edge of frame and
another on pin stem

66
UNKNOWN MAKER
Probably French
Pendant-brooch with a marsh fairy,
about 1900
Gold, enamel, and amethyst
9 x 3.7 x 0.8 cm (3⁹⁄₁₆ x 1⁷⁄₁₆ x ⁵⁄₁₆ in.)
Marks: Illegible impressed diamond on
reverse lower edge; owl with the letter *v* on
pin stem

67
PHILIPPE WOLFERS
Belgian, 1858-1929
"Night" pendant-brooch, about 1899
Gold, enamel, opal, pearl, and cast glass
7.4 x 3.2 x 0.8 cm (2¹⁵⁄₁₆ x 1¼ x ⁵⁄₁₆ in.)
Marks: The initials *P* and *W* in a cartouche in
an applied tab on reverse under owl; below
initials, *PW/EX:UNIQUE* in an applied plaque

68
EMMANUEL-JULES-JOSEPH (JOË) DESCOMPS
French, 1872-1948
For LÉON GARIOD, French
*Pendant necklace with a female head and a
sphinx*, about 1900

Gold, enamel, diamond, and pearl
Necklace: 33.4 cm (13⅛ in.) long
Pendant: 8.6 x 4.6 x 0.8 cm (3⅜ x 1¹³⁄₁₆ x
⁵⁄₁₆ in.)
Marks: Engraved *EJD* on lower part of
reverse; impressed diamond with the initials
L and *G* separated by a horn on spring ring;
eagle's head on bottom front

69
COMTE ENGUERRAND DU SUAU DE LA CROIX,
frame
French
LOUIS OSCAR ROTY, medal
French, 1846-1911
Wedding medallion, 1901
(medal designed in 1895)
Gilt silver, silver, enamel, diamond, and pearl
10.5 x 8.6 x 0.6 cm (4⅛ x 3⅜ x ¼ in.)
Marks: *CTE du Suau de la Croix* on lower
edge; boar's head on bottom right

70
LÉOPOLD ALBERT MARIN GAUTRAIT
French, 1865-1937
For LÉON GARIOD, French
Pendant-brooch with a female head,
about 1900
Gold, enamel, diamond, opal, and pearl
4 x 4.3 x 1.1 cm (1⁹⁄₁₆ x 1¹¹⁄₁₆ x ⁷⁄₁₆ in.)
Marks: *L. GAUTRAIT* on reverse; impressed dia-
mond with the initials *L* and *G* separated by a
horn on pin stem; eagle's head on pin stem

71
UNKNOWN MAKER
Possibly American
Pendant with a female profile head,
about 1900
Gold, silver, and enamel
Necklace: 35.6 cm (14 in.) long
Pendant: 4.2 x 0.3 cm (1⅝ x ⅛ in.)
Marks: Impressed *I.V.C.* along bottom edge;
impressed *AK* on front of bottom edge; two
eagles' heads, *no. 105*, and an impressed rhi-
noceros on jump ring of chain (chain and
pendant are by different makers)

72
UNKNOWN MAKER
French
Pendant-brooch with a fairy, about 1900
Gold and enamel
4.7 x 3.7 x 1.3 cm (1⅞ x 1⁷⁄₁₆ x ½ in.)
Marks: An eagle's head on pin stem and
another on armature hoop

73
UNKNOWN MAKER
French
Pendant-brooch with a female head,
about 1900
Platinum, gold, enamel, diamond, and ruby
4.5 x 5.4 x 1.1 cm (1¾ x 2⅛ x ⁷⁄₁₆ in.)
Marks: *WUST* on right corner on reverse;
eagle's head on right corner

74
ALIX ANGENOT
French
Purse, about 1900
Gold, silk, and metallic thread
16.5 x 18 x 1.2 cm (6½ x 7¹⁄₁₆ x ½ in.)
Marks: Impressed diamond with the initials *A*
and *A* separated by a pigeon; eagle's head on
purse frame; rhinoceros head on chain

75
CHARLES-RENÉ IHM
French
Hair comb–brooch with woman and peacock,
1901
Gold, enamel, opal, and tortoiseshell
13.5 x 6 x 1.2 cm (5⁵⁄₁₆ x 2⅜ x ½ in.)
Marks: Two owls on catch and pin stem

76
EMMANUEL-JULES-JOSEPH (JOË) DESCOMPS
French, 1872-1948
Pendant necklace with wood nymph, about
1900
Gold, enamel, diamond, pearl, and peridot
Necklace: 36.3 cm (14¹⁵⁄₁₆ in.) long
Pendant: 4.2 x 0.5 x 10.9 cm (1⅝ x ³⁄₁₆ x
4⁵⁄₁₆ in.)

Fig. 34. Victor Horta (Belgian, 1861-1947),
Bannister in the Hotel Solvay, Brussels, 1894

Marks: Impressed diamond with the initials *J* and *D* separated by a spider at bottom left of figure

77
UNKNOWN MAKER
Birth of Venus pendant, about 1900
Gold, enamel, and pearl
6.9 x 3.5 x 0.6 cm (2 11/16 x 1 3/8 x 1/4 in.)
Marks: Illegible mark on bail, possibly an owl

78
RIKER BROTHERS
American, working 1892–1926
Brooch with a female head with curvilinear tresses, about 1900
Gold, enamel, and diamond
2.1 x 2.7 x 0.7 cm (13/16 x 11/16 x 1/4 in.)
Marks: Impressed hallmark for Riker Brothers and *14 K* on reverse
Museum of Fine Arts, Boston. Gift of Dr. and Mrs. Joseph Sataloff 2007.634

79
VLADIMIR SOLOVIEV
Russian
For PETER CARL FABERGÉ
Russian, 1846–1920
Pendant locket with a female head in a ribbon frame, 1905–10
Gold, diamond, and ruby
8 x 4 x 0.7 cm (3 1/8 x 1 9/16 x 1/4 in.)
Marks: Impressed *BC* and *56MC* inside locket

Figure Illustrations

Fig. 1 (p. 4). DANTE GABRIEL ROSSETTI (English, 1828–1882), *Bocca Baciata (Lips That Have Been Kissed)*, 1859, oil on panel, 32.1 x 27 cm (12 5/8 x 1 5/8 in.), Museum of Fine Arts, Boston, Gift of James Lawrence, 1980.261

Fig. 2 (p. 10). SIR EDWARD COLEY BURNE-JONES (English, 1833–1898), *Hope*, 1896, oil on canvas, 179 x 63.5 cm (70 1/2 x 25 in.), Museum of Fine Arts, Boston, Given in memory of Mrs. George Marston Whitin by her four daughters, Mrs. Laurence Murray Keeler, Mrs. Sidney Russell Mason, Mrs. Elijah Kent Swift and Mrs. William Carey Crane, 40.778

Fig. 3 (p. 11). WILLIAM MORRIS (English, 1834–1896), *Length of furnishing fabric: "Cray,"* about 1884, block-printed cotton plain weave, 381 x 177.8 cm (150 x 70 in.), Museum of Fine Arts, Boston, Samuel Putnam Avery Fund and Ernest Kahn Fund, 2005.4

Fig. 4 (p. 12). UTAGAWA HIROSHIGE I (Japanese, 1797–1858), *The Iris Garden at Horikiri*, 1857, woodblock print, 33.8 x 22.2 cm (13 5/16 x 8 3/4 in.), Museum of Fine Arts, Boston, William Sturgis Bigelow Collection, 11.16827

Fig. 5 (p. 14). ODILON REDON (French, 1840–1916), *Centaur*, 1895–1900, pastel on canvas, 73 x 60.3 cm (28 3/4 x 23 3/4 in.), Museum of Fine Arts, Boston, Gift of Laurence K. Marshall, 64.2206

Fig. 6 (p. 15). LOUIS MAJORELLE (French, 1859–1926), *Cabinet*, about 1900, oak, stained walnut, Macassar ebony, burr walnut, burr amboyna, green-stained plane wood, palm wood, snakewood, coral-stained maple, wrought-iron mounts, and silk, 180 x 75 x 48 cm (70 7/8 x 29 1/2 x 18 7/8 in.), Museum of Fine Arts, Boston, Museum purchase with funds by exchange from the Elizabeth Day McCormick Collection, Gift of Mr. and Mrs. Edward Jackson Holmes, Gift of the Collection of Edward Jackson Holmes, Gift of Mrs. E. S. Hinds, Gift of Mrs. Guy Currier, Gift of Mrs. Edward Foote Dwight in memory of her father and mother George Parson and Sarah Elizabeth Eddy Parsons, Gift of the Misses Amy and Clara Curtis, Bequest of Mrs. Matilda E. Freylinghuysen, Gift of Paul and Helen Bernat, Harriet Otis Cruft Fund, George A. Goddard Fund, Gift of Mrs. George J. Putnam, Gift of Miss Anne C. Langdon in memory of her father Paul H. Langdon, Bequest of Susan Howard Pickering, Denman Waldo Ross Collection, Gift of Eben Howard Gay, Frederick Brown Fund, Gift of Eugene L. Garbáty, Bequest of Mrs. Charlotte Bradstreet, Bequest of Charles Hitchcock Taylor, Gift of Eleanor A. Sayre in memory of Miss Aimée and Miss Rosamond Lamb, Bequest of Mrs. Harriet J. Bradbury, Helen and Alice Colburn Fund, Francis Bartlett Donation, Gift of Frank Gair Macomber, Gift of George B. Dexter, an Anonymous Gift and Samuel Putnam Avery Fund, 2005.525

Fig. 7 (p. 16). VICTOR HORTA (Belgian, 1861–1947), *Staircase in the Horta House, rue Americaine, Brussels*, 1898–1901

Fig. 8 (p. 17). EMIL BIEBER (German, 1878–1962), *René Lalique and his wife Alice*, 1903, carbon print photograph, Musée d'Orsay, Paris

Fig. 9 (p. 19). JOSEF HOFFMANN (Austrian, 1870–1956), *Teapot*, 1904, silver, ebony, and raffia, 16.8 x 21.5 cm (6 5/8 x 8 7/16 in.), Museum of Fine Arts, Boston, Edwin E. Jack Fund, John H. and Ernestine A. Payne Fund, and Helen and Alice Colburn Fund, 1998.12

Fig. 10 (p. 20). EMILE GALLÉ (French, 1846–1904), *Vase*, 1891, cased and carved glass, 16.5 cm (6 1/2 in.) high, Museum of Fine Arts, Boston, Gift of Miss Mildred Kennedy, 53.1009

Fig. 11 (p. 23). ARAKI TOMEI (Japanese, 1817–1870), *Pair of menuki*, mid-late 19th century, gold, 2.4 x 0.7 cm (15/16 x 1/4 in.), Museum of Fine Arts, Boston, Charles Goddard Weld Collection, 11.5353a

Fig. 12 (p. 26). LÉON NIKOLAIEVITCH BAKST (Russian, 1866–1924), *The Butterfly (costume design for Anna Pavlova)*, 1913, watercolor and graphite pencil on paper, 28 x 45 cm (11 x 17 11/16 in.), Museum of Fine Arts, Boston, Gift of Mrs. John Munro Longyear and Mrs. Walter Scott Fitz, 14.701

Fig. 13 (p. 29). JAN TOOROP (Dutch, 1858–1929), *Delftsche Slaolie* (Delft Salad Oil), 1894, lithographic poster in color, 87.4 x 56 cm (34 7/16 x 22 1/16 in.), Museum of Fine Arts, Boston, Lee M. Friedman Fund, 1990.458

Fig. 14 (p. 30). LOUIS SAMSON II (French), *Covered ewer*, 1763, silver, 26.6 x 18.3 x 12.3 cm (10½ x 7 3/16 x 4 13/16 in.), Museum of Fine Arts, Boston, Elizabeth Parke Firestone and Harvey S. Firestone, Jr. Collection, 1993.254

Fig. 15 (p. 31). NELSON DAWSON (English, 1859-1942) and EDITH DAWSON (English), *Arts and Crafts waist ornament*, about 1905, silver, enamel, and turquoise, 27 x 4.9 cm (10½ x 1 15/16 in.), Tadema Gallery, London

Fig. 16 (p. 33). UTAGAWA HIROSHIGE I (Japanese, 1797-1858), *View of Matsuchiyama*, from the series *Famous Places in the Eastern Capital*, about 1840-42, woodblock print, 21.6 x 34 cm (8½ x 13⅜ in.), Museum of Fine Arts, Boston, William S. and John T. Spaulding Collection, 21.9782

Fig. 17 (p. 34). ALPHONSE MUCHA (Czechoslovakian, 1860-1939), *Art Nouveau–style vestibule from the Fouquet jewelry shop*, 1900-1910

Fig. 18 (p. 35). YOSHIOKA INABANOSUKE (Japanese), *Tsuba with design of peacock*, 18th century, *shakudō*, gold, and copper, 7.3 x 6.9 x 0.5 cm (2⅞ x 2 11/16 x 3/16 in.), Museum of Fine Arts, Boston, William Sturgis Bigelow Collection, 11.11689

Fig. 19 (p. 39). SARAH BERNHARDT (French, 1844-1923), *Fantastic inkwell (Self-portrait as a sphinx)*, 1880, bronze, 31.8 x 34.9 x 31.8 cm (12½ x 13¾ x 12½ in.), Museum of Fine Arts, Boston, Helen and Alice Colburn Fund, 1973.551

Fig. 20 (p. 40). ALPHONSE MUCHA (Czechoslovakian, 1860-1939), *La Dame aux Camelias / Sarah Bernhardt*, 1896, lithographic poster in color, 209.6 x 76.2 cm (82½ x 30 in.), Museum of Fine Arts, Boston, Gift of Mr. Charles Sumner Bird, 1970.514

Fig. 21 (p. 41). *Sarah Bernhardt wearing a Lalique headdress as Mélissande in "La Princesse lointaine,"* about 1895, photograph

Fig. 22 (p. 46). ARTHUR ILLIES (German, 1870-1952), *Jelänger-Jelieber (Honeysuckle)*, 1896, color etching on cream Asian paper, 55 x 35 cm (21⅝ x 13¾ in.), Museum of Fine Arts, Boston, Gift of John Goelet, 1998.101

Fig. 23 (p. 54). DAUM FRÈRES (French, established 1875), *Vase*, 1910-15, glass, 8.6 cm (3⅜ in.) high, Museum of Fine Arts, Boston, Bequest of Kathryn C. Buhler, 1987.48

Fig. 24 (p. 62). EUGÈNE GRASSET (French, born in Switzerland, 1841-1917), *Iris*, plate from *Plants and Their Application to Ornament*, 1897, illustrated book with 72 color lithographs, 45.6 x 33.6 cm (17 15/16 x 13¼ in.), Museum of Fine Arts, Boston, Gift of Ann Vershbow and Charles Beitz, 2004.2272

Fig. 25 (p. 71). E. A. SÉGUY, *Orchidées*, pochoir print, plate number 28 from *Les fleurs et leurs applications décoratives* (Paris: A. Calavas, 1902), Art and Architecture Collection, Miriam and Ira D. Wallach Division of Art, Prints and Photographs, The New York Public Library, Astor, Lenox and Tilden Foundations

Fig. 26 (p. 93). YOSHIMORI (Japanese), *Dragonflies and Grasses*, 1857, woodblock print, 31.9 x 10.4 cm (12 9/16 x 4⅛ in.), Museum of Fine Arts, Boston, Special Fund, 54.330

Fig. 27 (p. 98). UNKNOWN ARTIST (French), *Folding fan*, about 1905, silk satin leaf painted in watercolor, embroidered with sequins, with ivory sticks and steel rivet and ring, 42.5 cm (16¾ in.) wide, Museum of Fine Arts, Boston, Gift of H. Wade White, 53.2179

Fig. 28 (p. 103). WILLIAM H. BRADLEY (American, 1868-1962), *"The Modern Poster" for Scribner's*, 1895, relief process printed in color, 51 x 32 cm (20 1/16 x 12⅝ in.), Museum of Fine Arts, Boston, Anonymous gift in memory of John G. Pierce, Sr., 65.223

Fig. 29 (p. 108). OTTO ECKMANN (German, 1865-1902), *Fünf Schwane (Five Swans)*, 1897, tapestry-woven wool and cotton, 241.3 x 107.3 cm (95 x 42¼ in.), Museum of Fine Arts, Boston, Otis Norcuss Fund, Textile Curator's Fund, Charles Potter Kling Fund, and Textile Purchase Fund, 1991.440

Fig. 30 (p. 118). LÉON NIKOLAIEVITCH BAKST (Russian, 1866-1924), *Madame Bartet as Bérénice*, 1913, watercolor, gouache, gold paint, and graphite pencil on paper, 48.9 x 33.3 cm (19¼ x 13⅛ in.), Museum of Fine Arts, Boston, Gift of Mrs. John Munro Longyear and Mrs. Walter Scott Fitz, 14.403

Fig. 31 (p. 130). JAN TOOROP (Dutch, 1858-1928), *Panis Angelicus*, 1894, pastel, applied wet, over graphite on tan wove paper, 18.1 x 18.2 cm (7⅛ x 7 3/16 in.), Museum of Fine Arts, Boston, Gift of Jessie H. Wilkinson–Jessie H. Wilkinson Fund, 1993.535

Fig. 32 (p. 139). WILLIAM H. BRADLEY (American, 1868-1962), *Poster for Bradley—His Book (Woman and Blue Peacock)*, 1896, relief process printed in color, 121.9 x 86.4 x 2.5 cm (48 x 34 x 1 in.), Museum of Fine Arts, Boston, Lee M. Friedman Fund, 69.1152

Fig. 33 (p. 151). MURAKAMI JOCHIKU (Japanese, died about 1790-1800), *Tsuba with design of dragonfly and suisen (narcissus)*, late 18th–early 19th century, *shakudō*, gold, *shibuichi*, and shell, 7.5 x 7 x 0.6 cm (2 15/16 x 2¾ x ¼ in.), Museum of Fine Arts, Boston, Gift of John T. Spaulding, 37.1133

Fig. 34 (p. 159). VICTOR HORTA (Belgian, 1861-1947), *Bannister in the Hotel Solvay, Brussels*, 1894

Endleaves. WILLIAM MORRIS (English, 1834-1896), *Length of furnishing fabric: "Tulip,"* design registered 1875, block-printed cotton plain weave (chintz), 67.9 x 152.4 cm (26¾ x 60 in.), Museum of Fine Arts, Boston, Gift of Mr. and Mrs. Harold A. Pitman, 45.822b

GLOSSARY OF JEWELRY TERMS

Toni Strassler

bail. The loop on top of a pendant through which the chain passes.

baroque pearl. A natural or cultured, freshwater or saltwater pearl that is usually rounded and irregular in shape.

bezel-set. A descriptive term for a gem, enamel, or other object that is surrounded and held in place by a perfectly fitted rim of metal (the bezel) attached to a metal base and bent over slightly.

blister pearl. A natural half-pearl that develops irregularly when a boring worm or parasite pierces an oyster's shell and attaches itself to the inner surface of the shell.

cabochon. An unfaceted stone whose top side is cut and polished smooth into a convex form, usually with a flat bottom.

cabochonné. A variation of *cloisonné* enameling that imitates the look of cabochons by building up the enamel so that it is rounded within each of the small compartments outlined by the *cloisonné* wires.

casting. The process of forming an object by pouring molten metal or glass into a mold and letting it harden into the desired shape, which can then be removed from the mold.

champlevé. An enameling technique in which the metal background is dug out by etching, carving, or casting, forming recessed compartments into which enamels are placed, fused by heat, and then polished to produce a flat surface.

channel-set. A descriptive term for gems that have been set within two vertical metal walls without the use of metal to separate the individual stones.

chasing. The process of ornamenting the front of sheet or cast metal by using tools such as hammers, chisels, and punches to indent the surface of the metal, forming a raised design.

cloisonné. An enameling technique in which the design is outlined by flat metal wires adhered to a metal back, forming compartments that are filled with colored enamels, which are then fused by heat. Successive layers of enamel can be built up.

corsage ornament. An elaborate decoration designed in hinged or joined parts for flexibility and meant to be worn at the waist or on the bodice of a woman's dress.

dog collar. A broad, decorated necklace that fits tightly around the neck.

enamel. A material produced by using heat to fuse glass powder or grains colored by metal oxides, usually onto metal or glass, to produce a shiny surface. Enamel ranges from transparent to opaque and has been used for centuries in a variety of decorative techniques.

engraving. The process of creating a design by carving or cutting incisions into metal, glass, or other material.

en tremblant. An effect created when a piece of jewelry is mounted on spiral metal springs, allowing the ornament to quiver as the wearer moves. Also, the term for the mount itself.

faceted. The shape of a stone whose surfaces have been cut in a systematic arrangement of flat planes that catch and reflect light.

faience. A quartz-based ceramic covered with a vitreous glaze.

low relief. A design that is carved or molded to project only slightly from a flat surface.

mabe pearl. A cultured half-spherical pearl created by inserting a half-sphere-shaped mother-of-pearl nucleus into an oyster and attaching it to the flat part of the shell's inner surface.

pâte de verre. A technique in which usually opaque glass is ground and fired inside a mold, giving the appearance of a gemstone. The glass can then be lightly enameled.

patination. The staining of metal, glass, horn, or another surface, sometimes by the use of colored enamels.

plique à jour. A technique of enameling that, like *cloisonné*, uses metal partitions between the enamels, but in this case without a metal backing. The backless design allows light to pass through transparent and translucent colors.

repoussé. The process of producing a relief design in a thin piece of metal by using tools to stretch the metal from the back. Often used with chasing.

steatite. A brown or grayish green type of talc, a soft mineral. Also known as soapstone.

suite. A matching set of jeweled ornaments, usually including a necklace, brooch, earrings, bracelet, ring, and occasionally hair accessories.

NOTES

Art Nouveau Jewelry: An Overview

1. Unknown reviewer, quoting Hepworth Dixon's translation of an exhibition catalogue by Gustave Kahn, in "The Exhibition of Jewellery by René Lalique," *The Studio* 35 (1905): 130.

2. Burne-Jones was not part of the original Brotherhood but a follower of Rossetti.

3. Arnold Hauser, *A Social History of Art*, trans. Stanley Godman (London: Routledge and Kegan Paul, 1951), 2:821.

4. For the influences of Ruskin, Morris, and the British Arts and Crafts movement on Art Nouveau artists, see Stephan Tschudi Madsen, *Sources of Art Nouveau* (New York: DaCapo Press, 1975).

5. This was also the case with Louis Comfort Tiffany in the United States. His early ornaments, from the first decade of the twentieth century, feature dragonflies, dandelions, and Queen Anne's lace. See John Loring, *Louis Comfort Tiffany at Tiffany & Co.* (New York: Harry N. Abrams, 2002), 22–23, 26–27.

6. Joe Earle, *Splendors of Imperial Japan: Arts of the Meiji Period from the Khalili Collection* (London: Khalili Family Trust, 2002), 78.

7. Although Bing's gallery is often credited with coining the term for the new style, the name actually derives from a group of avant-garde artists in Brussels who, in 1884, were described as the "votaries of Art Nouveau" in the magazine *L'Art moderne*. See Stephen Escritt, *Art Nouveau* (London: Phaidon Press, 2000), 6.

8. Bing had visited the United States in 1894 in order to assess the state of the arts in the country. During his time there, he toured the workshops of Louis Comfort Tiffany and later became Tiffany's exclusive distributor in Europe. See Gabriel P. Weisberg, "Arts Ambassador for Europe and America," in Gabriel P. Weisberg, Edwin Becker, and Évelyne Possémé, eds., *The Origins of Art Nouveau: The Bing Empire* (Ithaca: Cornell University Press, 2004), 73–97.

9. For a discussion of the Bing workshops, see Gabriel Weisberg, "Redesigning the Home," in Weisberg, Becker, and Possémé, *The Origins of Art Nouveau*, 167–87.

10. Robert Goldwater, *Symbolism* (New York: Harper & Row, 1979), 6.

11. Although Art Nouveau artists rebelled against the recent Neoclassical art forms, they had an affinity for the eighteenth-century Rococo style, which celebrated nature and embraced asymmetrical, organic forms.

12. For the importance of line in Art Nouveau design, see Peter Selz and Mildred Constantine, *Art Nouveau: Art and Design at the Turn of the Century* (Garden City, NY: Doubleday, 1959), 10.

13. Paul Greenhalgh, "The Cult of Nature," in *Art Nouveau, 1890–1914*, ed. Paul Greenhalgh (London: V&A Publications, 2000), 61.

14. For the impact of technology on Art Nouveau artists, see Klaus-Jürgen Sembach, *Art Nouveau* (Cologne: Taschen, 2007), 8–15.

15. From the novel *Mort à crédit* (known in English as *Death on the Installment Plan*), as quoted in Victor Arwas, *Art Nouveau: The French Aesthetic* (London: Andreas Papadakis, 2002), 13.

16. The early-twentieth-century goods manufactured by the Newark firms of Unger Brothers and William B. Kerr Co. illustrate the attenuated Art Nouveau style preferred by American consumers. See Ulysses Dietz et al., *The Glitter and the Gold: Fashioning America's Jewelry* (Newark, NJ: Newark Museum, 1997), 86–93.

17. British Arts and Crafts jewelers also rebelled against the "tyranny of the diamond." Ruskin wrote, "The cutting of precious stones, in all ordinary cases, requires little exertion of any mental faculty; some tact and judgment in avoiding flaws, and so on, but nothing to bring out the whole mind. Every person who wears cut jewels merely for the sake of their value is, therefore, a slave-driver." See John Ruskin, *On Art and Life* (New York: Penguin Books, 2005), 21. (Originally published in "The Nature of Gothic," in Ruskin's *The Stones of Venice*, vol. 2 [1853].)

18. In Britain, the taste for all-white jewels made of platinum and diamond would continue through the reign of Edward VII (r. 1901–1910). The style was widely copied in the United States. While yellow gold was most popular among Art Nouveau jewelers, green and, occasionally, rose gold were also used. Green tones were achieved through the addition of cadmium, while rose tints were attained by adding copper.

19. Although *plique à jour* enameling was known during the Middle Ages and described by Benvenuto Cellini in his *Treatises*, the technique was lost for several centuries. It was reinvented by the French enamelist Riffault in 1867 and soon used by the jeweler Frédéric Boucheron. Other jewelers in France, Belgium, and the United States followed suit.

20. A bracelet of horn and silver by Lalique was exhibited in the Paris Salon of 1896. See Maria Teresa Gomes Ferreira, *Lalique bijoux* (Lisbon: Musée Calouste Gulbenkian, 1999), 44-45. For the influence of the Japanese use of horn and ivory on Lalique, see Jessica Hodge, *Lalique* (San Diego, CA: Thunder Bay Press, 1999), 12-13.

21. The Congo Free State was privately owned by Leopold II. His exploitation of the area and cruelty to the indigenous population were so egregious that he was forced to cede control to the Belgian government in 1908. For more information, see Nigel Cawthorne, *The World's Worst Atrocities* (London: Octopus Publishing Group, 1999).

22. *Pâte de verre* glass was perfected in the late nineteenth century by the French sculptor Henri Cros and was used extensively by the noted French glassmaker Emile Gallé. For more information on this technique and Lalique's experiments with glass in jewelry, see Clare Phillips, "Jewellery and the Art of the Goldsmith," in Greenhalgh, *Art Nouveau, 1890–1914*, 237-49.

23. For information on cut-steel ornaments in Great Britain and iron jewelry in Germany, see Anne Clifford, *Cut-Steel and Berlin Iron Jewellery* (South Brunswick and New York: A. S. Barnes, 1971).

Symbols and Motifs in Art Nouveau Jewelry

1. Jean Moréas, "Le Symbolisme," *Le Figaro*, September 18, 1886.

2. Theosophy was originated by Ukrainian-born Helena Petrovna Blavatsky in the 1870s; she cofounded the Theosophical Society in New York City in 1875. The Rosicrucian order was founded by the German Christian Rosenkreuz, who was born in 1378 and visited Damascus, Egypt, and Morocco, where he studied with the masters of the occult arts. In the mid-nineteenth century, it received new interest from occultist Eliphas Lévi (1810–1875), leading to the formation of the Qabalistic Order of the Rosy Cross in 1888.

3. An interest in séances began about the middle of the nineteenth century with the Fox sisters in the United States, who claimed to speak to the spirit world. Popular in Europe as well, séances were a parlor entertainment for most people, but they do illustrate a widespread interest in the spiritual world in the second half of the nineteenth century.

4. Steven Escritt, *Art Nouveau* (London: Phaidon, 2000), 21.

5. Emile Gallé, as quoted in Ghisalane Wood, *Art Nouveau and the Erotic* (New York: Harry N. Abrams, 2000), 70.

6. Joseph Purtell, *That Tiffany Touch* (New York: Random House, 1971), 145.

7. Vivienne Becker, *Art Nouveau Jewelry* (New York: E. P. Dutton, 1985), 17.

8. For further discussion of the female image in Art Nouveau jewelry, see Becker, *Art Nouveau Jewelry*.

9. For further information about the demimonde, see Joanna Richardson, *The Courtesans: The Demi-Monde in Nineteenth-Century France* (Cleveland: World Publishing Company, 1967; repr., London: Phoenix, 2000).

FURTHER READING

Arwas, Victor. *Art Nouveau: The French Aesthetic*. London: Andreas Papadakis, 2002.

Becker, Vivienne. *Art Nouveau Jewelry*. New York: E. P. Dutton, 1985.

Brunhammer, Yvonne, ed. *The Jewels of Lalique*. Paris: Flammarion, 1998.

Cerval, Marguerite de, ed. *Dictionnaire international du bijou*. Paris: Editions du Regard, 1998.

Dietz, Ulysses Grant, Jenna Weissman Joselit, Kevin J. Smead, and Janet Zapata. *The Glitter and the Gold: Fashioning America's Jewelry*. Newark, NJ: Newark Museum, 1997.

Duncan, Alastair. *Jewellery: The Designers A–K* and *Jewellery: The Designers L–Z*. Vols. 1 and 2 of *The Paris Salons, 1895–1914*. Woodbridge, Suffolk: Antique Collectors' Club, 1994.

Falk, Fritz. *Schmuck / Jewellery, 1840–1940: Highlights Schmuckmuseum Pforzheim*. Stuttgart: Arnoldsche, 2004.

——. *Schmuck-Kunst im Jugendstil / Art Nouveau Jewellery*. Stuttgart: Arnoldsche, 1999.

Gary, Marie-Noël de, ed. *Les Fouquet: Bijoutiers & joailliers à Paris, 1860–1960*. Paris: Musée des arts décoratifs, 1983.

Greenhalgh, Peter, ed. *Art Nouveau, 1890–1914*. London: V&A Publications, 2000.

Koch, Michael, et al. *The Belle Epoque of French Jewellery, 1850–1910*. London: Thomas Heneage, 1990.

Sataloff, Joseph. *Art Nouveau Jewelry*. Bryn Mawr: Dorrance & Company, 1984.

Van Strydonck de Burkel, Rolende, and Jacqueline Francotte-Florence. *Le bijou Art Nouveau en Europe*. Brussels: Editions Racine; Lausanne: Bibliothèque des Arts, 1998.

Vever, Henri. *French Jewelry of the Nineteenth Century*. Translated by Katherine Purcell. London: Thames & Hudson, 2001. Originally published as *La bijouterie française au XIXe siècle*, 3 vols. (Paris: H. Floury, 1906–8).

INDEX

Published in the United Kingdom in 2008 by

Lund Humphries
Gower House
Croft Road
Aldershot
Hampshire GU11 3HR

This book was published in conjunction with the exhibition "Imperishable Beauty: Art Nouveau Jewelry," organized by the Museum of Fine Arts, Boston.

Museum of Fine Arts, Boston
July 23–November 9, 2008

Cincinnati Art Museum
October 24, 2009–January 25, 2010

© 2008 by Museum of Fine Arts, Boston
This edition published by arrangement with MFA Publications, a division of the Museum of Fine Arts, Boston

www.lundhumphries.com

Lund Humphries is part of Ashgate Publishing

British Library Cataloging-in-Publication Data
A catalog record for this book is available from the British Library

ISBN 978-0-85331-997-9

Front cover: Charles Desrosiers, *Orchid brooch*, 1898–1901, detail (catalogue 20)
Back cover: René Lalique, *Carnation watch*, 1898–1900, detail (catalogue 6)

All illustrations in this book were photographed by Greg Heins of the Imaging Studios, Museum of Fine Arts, Boston, except where otherwise noted.

Manuscript edited by
Sarah McGaughey Tremblay
Copyedited by Dalia Geffen

Designed and produced by
Cynthia Rockwell Randall
Printed and bound at CS Graphics, Pte, Ltd.

FIRST EDITION
Printed in Singapore
This book was printed on acid-free paper.

PHOTOGRAPHY AND COPYRIGHT CREDITS

All works by Georges Fouquet, René Lalique, and Alphonse Mucha are © 2008 Artists Rights Society (ARS), New York / ADAGP, Paris.

All works by Victor Horta are © 2008–Victor Horta - SOFAM Belgium.

All illustrations in this book were photographed by Greg Heins and the Imaging Studios, Museum of Fine Arts, Boston, except for the following:

Fig. 7: © Horta House, Rue Americaine, Brussels, Belgium / Paul Maeyaert / The Bridgeman Art Library

Fig. 8: Photo: Hervé Lewandowski / Réunion des Musées Nationaux / Art Resource, NY

Fig. 15: Courtesy, Tadema Gallery, London

Fig. 17: Artwork © Mucha Trust / ADAGP, Paris; image © Archivo Iconografico, S.A. / CORBIS

Fig. 21: Photo by Bob Thomas / Popperfoto / Getty Images

Fig. 25: Courtesy, New York Public Library

Fig. 34: © Hotel Solvay, Brussels, Belgium / The Bridgeman Art Library